SpringerBriefs in Education

We are delighted to announce SpringerBriefs in Education, an innovative product type that combines elements of both journals and books. Briefs present concise summaries of cutting-edge research and practical applications in education. Featuring compact volumes of 50 to 125 pages, the SpringerBriefs in Education allow authors to present their ideas and readers to absorb them with a minimal time investment. Briefs are published as part of Springer's eBook Collection. In addition, Briefs are available for individual print and electronic purchase.

SpringerBriefs in Education cover a broad range of educational fields such as: Science Education, Higher Education, Educational Psychology, Assessment & Evaluation, Language Education, Mathematics Education, Educational Technology, Medical Education and Educational Policy.

SpringerBriefs typically offer an outlet for:

- An introduction to a (sub)field in education summarizing and giving an overview of theories, issues, core concepts and/or key literature in a particular field
- A timely report of state-of-the art analytical techniques and instruments in the field of educational research
- A presentation of core educational concepts
- An overview of a testing and evaluation method
- A snapshot of a hot or emerging topic or policy change
- An in-depth case study
- A literature review
- A report/review study of a survey
- An elaborated thesis

Both solicited and unsolicited manuscripts are considered for publication in the SpringerBriefs in Education series. Potential authors are warmly invited to complete and submit the Briefs Author Proposal form. All projects will be submitted to editorial review by editorial advisors.

SpringerBriefs are characterized by expedited production schedules with the aim for publication 8 to 12 weeks after acceptance and fast, global electronic dissemination through our online platform SpringerLink. The standard concise author contracts guarantee that:

- an individual ISBN is assigned to each manuscript
- each manuscript is copyrighted in the name of the author
- the author retains the right to post the pre-publication version on his/her website or that of his/her institution

Michelle Trudgett · Susan Page · Rhonda Povey · Michelle Locke
Editors

Indigenous Early Career Researchers in Australian Universities

Our Stories

Editors
Michelle Trudgett
Western Sydney University
Parramatta, NSW, Australia

Susan Page
Western Sydney University
Parramatta, NSW, Australia

Rhonda Povey
Western Sydney University
Parramatta, NSW, Australia

Michelle Locke
Western Sydney University
Kingswood, NSW, Australia

ISSN 2211-1921 ISSN 2211-193X (electronic)
SpringerBriefs in Education
ISBN 978-981-97-2822-0 ISBN 978-981-97-2823-7 (eBook)
https://doi.org/10.1007/978-981-97-2823-7

© The Editor(s) (if applicable) and The Author(s) 2025. This book is an open access publication.

Open Access This book is licensed under the terms of the Creative Commons Attribution 4.0 International License (http://creativecommons.org/licenses/by/4.0/), which permits use, sharing, adaptation, distribution and reproduction in any medium or format, as long as you give appropriate credit to the original author(s) and the source, provide a link to the Creative Commons license and indicate if changes were made.

The images or other third party material in this book are included in the book's Creative Commons license, unless indicated otherwise in a credit line to the material. If material is not included in the book's Creative Commons license and your intended use is not permitted by statutory regulation or exceeds the permitted use, you will need to obtain permission directly from the copyright holder.

The use of general descriptive names, registered names, trademarks, service marks, etc. in this publication does not imply, even in the absence of a specific statement, that such names are exempt from the relevant protective laws and regulations and therefore free for general use.

The publisher, the authors and the editors are safe to assume that the advice and information in this book are believed to be true and accurate at the date of publication. Neither the publisher nor the authors or the editors give a warranty, expressed or implied, with respect to the material contained herein or for any errors or omissions that may have been made. The publisher remains neutral with regard to jurisdictional claims in published maps and institutional affiliations.

This Springer imprint is published by the registered company Springer Nature Singapore Pte Ltd.
The registered company address is: 152 Beach Road, #21-01/04 Gateway East, Singapore 189721, Singapore

If disposing of this product, please recycle the paper.

We dedicate this book to Emeritus Professor Dr. MaryAnn Bin-Sallik who was the first Indigenous Australian to be employed full-time in the Australian higher education sector. Amongst her long list of outstanding accomplishments, she was also the first Indigenous Australian person to earn a Doctoral qualification from Harvard University. A trailblazer who was responsible for editing a book titled Aboriginal Women by Degrees: Their Stories of the Journey Towards Academic Achievement. Released in 2000, this collection of stories provided our editorial team with much inspiration to compile this book which, similar to Bin-Sallik's flagship manuscript, also offers the stories of a number of Indigenous academics who have navigated their own pathways in higher education. Professor Bin-Sallik, we offer this dedication with deep respect, awe, and gratitude for all you have contributed to the sector for many decades.

Preface

Indigenous Australian Early Career Researchers enrich the academy through their expertise, their teaching, and research, and critically through their Indigenous Knowledges and connections to community. The Early Career Researcher (ECR) label, which commonly refers to a five-to-seven-year period after the awarding of doctoral qualifications, often obscures years of experience Indigenous scholars have amassed in their communities and work. Indeed, some of the ECRs whose stories you will read in this book had worked for many years in universities while they completed their doctorates, while others were relatively new to the academy, having come to their doctoral studies much earlier in their professional lives or from professional pathways. All have navigated the predominant whiteness of our Australian university systems. The book explores key barriers and facilitators to advancing a meaningful and fulfilling academic career in the higher education sector for Australian Indigenous doctoral graduates. We envisage that the book will be of interest to many people working in universities in Australia and internationally and anticipate the stories will be of particular interest to Indigenous ECRs and to faculty and university leaders.

We expect the Indigenous ECR narratives shared here will encourage readers to consider their own institutional practices and how university policies and practices impede or enable parity and success in the sector. If you are a supervisor of Indigenous ECRs in your workplace, the chapters in the book will deepen your understanding of the issues that are important to Indigenous ECRs, the challenges the ECR might encounter in building their postdoctoral careers, as well as the aspirations the ECR might bring to their work. For policymakers eager to develop successful Indigenous researchers who can contribute to institutional effectiveness, there are clear and obvious directives for action. That these narratives are shared by a diverse range of ECRs at different career stages, from a variety of institutions and an array of disciplines and professional backgrounds, suggesting a robustness of message that should hearten the reader seeking to effect change.

This book arose from an Australian Research Council-funded project, *Developing Indigenous Australian Early Career Researchers* (Trudgett & Page, 2019–2021) which set out to explore the career trajectories of Indigenous Australian scholars in the early period following completion of doctoral studies. The Indigenous ECR project builds on previous work examining the experiences of Indigenous people who had successfully completed doctoral students undertaken by Trudgett and Page, along with then colleague, Associate Professor Neil Harrison (Trudgett, Page & Harrison 2016) and Trudgett's own doctoral work (Trudgett, 2013). Exploration of the early career period for Indigenous people who had completed doctorates seemed a logical next step, as universities aim to build on the growing numbers of Indigenous peoples completing doctoral qualifications.

The resultant *Developing Indigenous Australian ECRs* project was a longitudinal study in which ECRs who participated in the study were interviewed once a year, over three years, with a view to exploring enablers and barriers to their work and career success. In the spirit of the grant, we included a position for an ECR as part of the grant funding. It seemed appropriate to create a position for an Indigenous postdoctoral fellow and given the grant holders senior positions, a research officer also seemed sensible. Luckily, two recently completed Ph.D. students (Locke and Povey), who we (Trudgett/Page) had supervised, were able to join the team. It was a great way to provide opportunities for two doctoral graduates at different stages in their own careers, with the added bonus that we knew we could all work together. The idea for the book emerged as we were thinking about creative and useful ways to disseminate and share findings from the project. Creating a career opportunity for our ECR project participants seemed like a beneficial, engaging way of augmenting the usual refereed publications that are expected to flow from a funded research project.

The possibility of contributing a chapter to an edited volume was canvassed in the initial and subsequent year interviews. The option to contribute a chapter to an edited book was discussed with participants from the early stages of the research and was included as part of the written information for participants. After the third and final round of interviews was completed, we formally invited each person to contribute a chapter to a collection of stories outlining the career journeys of Indigenous ECRs. Fittingly, Dr. Locke, the ECR undertaking postdoctoral work on the study also contributed a chapter. We started the project with 30 amazing Indigenous ECRs involved in the study and by the end of the third year, 28 ECRs were still with us. Health reasons prevented two ECRs from continuing in the study. The research team is grateful for the contributions of all the ECRs to the study and to the 15 ECRs for whom this was the right time to write a chapter.

Each chapter in the book, whether written as an academic essay, personal reflection, narrative or an Indigenous story, is authored by an Indigenous ECR. We emphasised the voluntary nature of contributing a chapter and encouraged the ECRs to use their interview transcripts as a prompt and to potentially save them some time in preparation of their manuscripts. While we did have a broad structure for the book, based on a career trajectory, the ECRs were given a wide brief to contribute reflective works that could be as scholarly or as creative as they wished. As you will see, our scholars took to this remit with gusto, incorporating Indigenous storytelling, poetry, metaphor and analogy. Some authors addressed their fellow ECRs while others addressed their comments to their non-Indigenous colleagues and university leaders. Contributors explore, analyse, explain, and reflect on the interplay between themselves as individual agents, the local institutional culture, and their own perceptions of and expected ECR career trajectory. There is an immediacy to these reflective stories that is rarely captured in the disaggregated and de-identified 'data' which is the (necessary) foundation of the qualitative journal papers which have resulted from this study.

The stories on the following pages are replete with the wisdom that is borne of experience, of having done the 'hard yards' and now having a tale to tell. Each is a unique personal account and yet there are recurring themes and feelings, some are palpably angry, and many reflect a deep frustration with systems that are challenging to navigate and environments which are sometimes indifferent and occasionally hostile. Sadly, some are resigned to the slow pace of change in our institutions and the lack of recognition of Indigenous work, yet there is also a sense of hope. The stories bristle with Indigenous agency. They are exemplars of tenacity, humour, excellence, and success—often in the face of adversity. The reflective nature of many of the stories generates multiple insights, illuminating a path for other Indigenous ECRs to follow, hopefully with fewer obstacles and a swathe of hints for how to find the kind of support necessary to navigate a successful career trajectory. Each story is also a lesson for those in universities who are responsible for the career development of Indigenous ECR. Some authors make those lessons explicit, others require the reader to walk alongside the author and read carefully for the cues, as might occur when Elders are teaching the inexperienced.

The Structure of the Book

The book begins and ends with contextual chapters authored by the editorial team, and frame the chapters authored by Indigenous ECRs. The Introduction outlines the colonial context of Indigenous participation in Australian universities, while the concluding chapter considers possibilities for the future, and in a call to action, invites readers to actively engage with the Indigenous community to make Australian universities a place where Indigenous success is supported, promoted, and celebrated. The ECR authored chapters are organised into three parts: *Transitions and Expectations*; *Navigation*; and *Aspirations*. This sequence takes the reader from the early ECR phase of shifting away from doctoral student, to how to navigate that transition and finally to an illumination of the variety of aspirations Indigenous ECRs have for their careers, themselves and their communities. The chapters can be read consecutively but can also be read out of sequence. Each story is encapsulated, engaging the reader on its own terms, defining success individually and collectively and offering solutions to challenges in a generous spirit, with the expectation that readers will hear and act.

Introduction

The Introduction, authored by the editorial team, outlines Indigenous participation in Australian higher education, giving a brief overview of some key touchpoints since the colonial era. This historical synopsis provides a context for the Indigenous ECR narratives that follow and acts as a call to action and a marshalling of institutional intent to capitalise on the hard-won successes borne of growing Indigenous doctoral success. To squander the opportunity to greater and more meaningful contributions by Indigenous peoples to higher education, would be to diminish the prospects of enhanced Indigenous research, quality of teaching and modelling for Indigenous students that flow from highly qualified and skilled Indigenous scholars. The benefits to Indigenous communities and the nation are considerable.

Transitions and Expectations

Dr. Vinnitta Mosby outlines a compelling story of how success can occur when critical elements are aligned. Dr. Mosby's doctoral success led to an unanticipated role as an early career academic working in the university where her doctorate was completed. Concerns about climate change and its effects on Torres Strait Islander peoples were the driving force behind her doctoral work, rather than the desire to become an academic. Doctoral success came from hard work plus a combination of excellent honours results, a strong supervision team, who worked well together and an unexpected encounter with a visiting international Indigenous scholar who bolstered both confidence and knowledge. Dr. Mosby also reminds us of the value of the financial freedom a scholarship enables and how nurturing family support can be on such a long academic journey.

Dr. Robyn Ober's chapter illuminates a career trajectory from teacher education practice in rural, remote and metropolitan schools which came full circle when she returned to Bachelor Institute, where she had done her initial teacher training course, to teach a new generation of educators. Dr. Ober reminds us of value of research mentorship, initially as she learned alongside more experienced researchers and later as she experienced the satisfaction of mentoring Indigenous students in their own learning journeys. She outlines the importance of Indigenous leaders and role models to show the possibilities in doctoral education and equally shows the significance of sharing the often-lengthy doctoral journey, with Indigenous colleagues. Dr. Ober also highlights the strangeness of finishing such a large undertaking and the sudden shift to the rigours of a scholarly life of teaching, publishing and generally being in demand.

Associate Professor Katrina Thorpe's chapter takes the form of a letter offering pragmatic advice about how to get the best out of the postdoctoral period and reflecting on the gap between expectations and the realities of what is possible to achieve. Associate Professor Thorpe encourages her fellow ECRs to follow their passion and to enjoy the postdoctoral time to focus on building or enhancing a research profile. She offers sage advice about the importance of saying no to distractions by creating clear boundaries bolstered by a strong sense of the value of the research that Indigenous researchers are undertaking. On a very practical note, Associate Professor Thorpe offers guidance about vital questions to ask when you have research funding. While the focus of the chapter is on Indigenous ECRs, there are also recommendations to universities about the value of developing post PhD pathways for HDR students in your own institutions.

Navigation

Dr. Michelle Locke explores the challenges of being 'first in family', while also recognising the enormous support of her family and the collective pride in her success. Dr. Locke charts a circuitous route to academic work via a profession, noting the importance of learning environments which nurture and support Indigenous Ph.D. candidates. The COVID-19 pandemic affected Dr. Locke, in the practical ways that impacted many others, but she also shares the vulnerability and loss of confidence that can attend the isolation wrought by pandemic lockdowns. Dr. Locke illuminates how the challenges of learning the language of academia can be both a barrier and once learned a form of entry. Central to Dr. Locke's chapter is the importance of publishing, along with the weight of responsibility for ensuring that Indigenous voices are both valued through careful data analysis and amplified by thoughtful publishing.

Dr. Tracy Woodroffe reflects thoughtfully on a younger self who burned with a sense of urgency to get her research done and illuminates the often messy and nonlinear nature of research. The chapter explores building a track record in the postdoctoral phase, and how to combine prior professional experience to build a new academic career. Along the way, Dr. Woodroffe explains the unsettling professional identity challenge that accompanied the transition to an academic life after a successful and rewarding professional career. Dr. Woodroffe also reminds us of the value of curiosity and trusting that pursuing what interests you will lead to somewhere interesting, even if it wasn't what you intended. Finally, Dr. Woodroffe offers some sage advice about the constant challenge to prioritise family life and balance academic work.

Dr. Vincent Backhaus argues persuasively and eloquently that being an Indigenous ECR has a particularity not shared with all ECRs, given that Indigenous teaching and research are so intimately intertwined with who we are as Indigenous people and the histories and contemporary experiences of our peoples. Dr. Backhaus reminds us that Indigenous ECRs act with agency and are often pioneers in their fields, forging fresh pathways into the academy, accompanied by uncertainty and the risk of constantly making mistakes. Also considered are issues of identity, not just Indigeneity but developing emerging professional identities, as well. Dr. Backhaus recognises the privilege but also the significant responsibility of being an Indigenous ECR, benefitting from opportunities unknown to our forebears.

Dr. Anthony McKnight's chapter is infused with stories of lessons from Elders and family. Dr. McKnight explains that the chapter might be confusing for some readers, reflecting his own academic journey and mirroring the way Elders often indirectly guide community through convoluted stories. We see an example of Aunty pedagogy and the capacity to maintain connection through discourse. The chapter is a powerful insight into the intersecting tensions between not forgetting where you come from, latent community fear of losing their young people to Western education systems, and community expectations and the responsibility of being an Indigenous person doing doctoral work. Using that most ordinary, everyday item, the humble potato chip, Dr. McKnight seeks to distil his experiences and lessons learned into an instructive poem.

Dr. Skye Akbar provides wise advice for new Indigenous ECRs in the hope that her hard-won experience will help others to navigate a system in which there are inherent challenges of being the first or only Indigenous academic at a time when Indigenous expertise is in significant demand, with too few people to fill institutional requirements. Dr. Akbar explores some of the common pitfalls for Indigenous ECRs who find themselves in foreign institutional environments where the demands for their expertise are not always in the Indigenous ECRs' best interest for career development or meeting community needs. Learning to distinguish which opportunities will be fruitful and which will simply take you away from your own priorities, is critical, but doesn't necessarily come with a handbook. Dr. Akbar encourages readers to choose what will advance your career and your community.

Professor Scott Avery has crafted a beautiful allegory, which compellingly combines narratives of Country (ocean), wisdom of Elders and intersectionality. The cultural vibrance of the story is juxtaposed with a thorough meditation on the risks and (occasional) benefits of representing two diversity 'ticked boxes'. Professor Avery very incisively deploys a football metaphor to characterise his context and tackles head on the question of capacity. He asks challenging questions about who has the right to speak, actively contexts disciplinary approaches that seek to contain and restrain and calls out institutional practices that assume knowledge and decision-making primacy. Professor Avery also pays respect to Elders and to the advocacy which has opened up university spaces to Indigenous people.

Dr. BJ Newton's chapter is addressed to Indigenous ECR colleagues who might be starting out in their postdoctoral careers. Dr. Newton outlines 8 rules for surviving academia for ECRs. The chapter also touched on the benefits and pitfalls of taking up a leadership role in the ECR period. The 'rules' cover advice for self, advice about how and who to collaborate with, and the potential for a greater good. Dr. Newton suggest that knowing your own values and priorities will help to guide both what you do and what you don't do and help you to pursue your own research. Finding culturally nurturing environments, respectful collaborator and trustworthy leaders can help you to build the next phase of your career. Driving outcomes for the next generation of Indigenous researchers is a rewarding aspect of your newfound leadership.

Aspirations

Professor Tristan Kennedy examines and reflects upon the role and potential value of formal and informal mentorship for Indigenous ECRs. He highlights the collegiality and collaboration of Indigenous mentorship, but points to the current scarcity of senior Indigenous scholars which can make it more challenging to find an Indigenous mentor to help develop that next part of a career. Professor Kennedy explores the pitfalls of institutional mentorship programmes which are developed by and feature non-Indigenous people, with worthwhile insights for programme developers who want to support the career trajectories of Indigenous ECRs. His steadfast rebuttal of Indigenous deficiency is refreshing and should be a guide for non-Indigenous readers concerned with Indigenous career development.

Professor Corrinne Sullivan's chapter juxtaposes raw talent, absolute determination and sheer will to 'do more' with the barely visible structures and attitudes designed to keep Indigenous people 'in their place'. Reflecting on a career journey that spans schooling to the achievement of a senior academic role, Professor Sullivan charts a recurring theme of underestimation, first in her family and later in her workplaces. She sagely uses this underestimation to refute low expectations, whether winning awards for her honours and doctoral work, or accolades for her research. As well, Professor Sullivan powerfully illustrates the connection between 'dreaming big', individual agency and how opportunities seized can build momentum for the next career goal. A key lesson from this chapter is not to underestimate Indigenous ability, particularly where early signs of success demonstrate ample prospect of future possibilities, but rather to create opportunity for talent to flourish.

Dr. Marcelle Townsend-Cross' work is driven by her commitment to social justice for Indigenous people, which drives her Indigenous Studies teaching research. This chapter sends a clear message to universities that providing creative and innovative options for Indigenous scholars can result in retaining talent, underlining the value of supporting Indigenous ECRs as they develop their new professional identities. Dr. Townsend-Cross also highlights the importance of finding like-minded collaborators who can help to navigate the institutional and research practices that are not always known to Indigenous ECRs. Collaborators and mentors can help to demystify processes such as journal publishing and can lead to further invitations, bolstering opportunity and reputation. Dr. Townsend-Cross reminds us of the critical role of journal reviewers and editors in supporting the development of beginning scholars.

Dr. Melinda Mann's reflective chapter begins where all learning begins, in childhood. Dr. Mann's rich analogy, illustrating Indigenous ways of being, knowing and doing draws on a story of fishing. The story deftly incorporates ways of learning about place and identity, and foundations for theorising about cognition, along with lessons about patience, useful in later life for withstanding the rigors of academic life. Her chapter identifies with pinpoint accuracy the time in primary school when racism began to challenge, though not deter, her learning, imagination and aspirations. The critical importance of mentors, Indigenous centres in universities, as well as friends and family are clearly demonstrated. This chapter is a narrative of resilience, resistance and a ponderance of the question of regret, offset by the unexpected joy of witnessing the strategic use of the title doctor by community members, undoubtedly proud of their member.

Future Directions

The final chapter, authored by **Dr. Michelle Locke**, concludes the book with a discussion of the possibilities for the future. Echoing the call for action from the first chapter and resonating with the multiple voices of the Indigenous ECRs, Dr. Locke asks readers, particularly those non-Indigenous readers with authority and opportunity in universities, to heed the invitation to take responsibility and join with Indigenous colleagues to make universities places where Indigenous ECRs can realistically build on the strength and success that guided them through doctoral programmes to curate fulfilling careers that contribute to Indigenous community and national success.

Parramatta, Australia   Prof. Susan Page

References

Trudgett, M. (2013). Stop, Collaborate and Listen: A Guide to Seeding Success for Indigenous Higher Degree Research Students. In R.G. Craven & J. Mooney (Eds.), *Seeding Success in indigenous Australian Higher Education (Diversity in Higher Education)* (pp. 137–155). Emerald Group Publishing Limited.

Trudgett, M., Page, S., & Harrison, N. (2016). Brilliant minds: A snapshot of successful Indigenous Australian doctoral students. *The Australian Journal of Indigenous Education, 45*(1), 70–79.

Developing Indigenous Australian Early Career Researchers Project Publications

Locke, M.L., Trudgett, M., & Page, S. (2021). Indigenous early career researchers—Creating pearls in the academy. *Australian Educational Researcher.* https://doi.org/10.1007/s13384-021-00485-1

Locke, M.L., Trudgett, M., & Page, S. (2022). Australian Indigenous early career researchers: Unicorns, cash cows and performing monkeys. *Race Ethnicity and Education.* https://doi.org/10.1080/13613324.2022.2114445

Locke, M.L., Trudgett, M., & Page, S. (2022) Beyond the doctorate: Exploring Indigenous early career research trajectories. *The Australian Journal of Indigenous Education.* https://ajie.atsis.uq.edu.au/ajie/issue/current

Locke, M.L., Trudgett, M., & Page, S. (2022) Building and Strengthening Indigenous early career researcher trajectories. *Higher Education Research and Development.* https://doi.org/10.1080/07294360.2022.2048637

Locke, M., Trudgett, M., & Page, S. (2022). Indigenous early career researchers in the time of Covid-19. *Journal of Australian Indigenous Issues, 25*(3–4), 11–27. https://search.informit.org/doi/10.3316/informit.881818329736230

Locke, M., Trudgett, M., & Page, S. (2024). All hands on deck: Coordinated approaches to Indigenous early career development. *The International Indigenous Policy Journal, 15*(2). https://doi.org/10.18584/iipj.2024.15.2.15182

Locke, M., Trudgett, M., & Page, S. (2024). Indigenous early career researcher's perspectives of 'safe spaces' in higher education. *The Australian Journal of Education, 68*(3), 161–175. https://doi.org/10.1177/00049441241274522

Povey, R., Trudgett, M., Page, S., Locke, M.L., & Harry, M. (2022). Raising an Indigenous academic community: A strength-based approach to Indigenous early career mentoring in higher education. *Australian Educational Researcher.* https://doi.org/10.1007/s13384-022-00542-3

Povey, R., Trudgett, M., Page, S., & Locke, M. L. (2023). Hidden in plain view: Indigenous early career researchers' experiences and perceptions of racism in Australian universities. *Critical Studies in Education.* https://doi.org/10.1080/17508487.2022.2159469

Acknowledgements

Many incredible pioneers have paved the way in Indigenous education, making it possible for this book to come to life. We acknowledge their intellectual contributions and sustained advocacy throughout several decades, often staged on the front line of a battleground underpinned by institutional and structural racism. While considerable challenges remain, Indigenous Early Career Researchers enter an academy changed by the work of these courageous scholars and professional staff.

We would also like to acknowledge our families who have provided tireless support throughout the book's conception and editorial process. Your ongoing belief in our work is essential to the success of this book.

Finally, we sincerely thank the authors for their valuable contributions. Each of you has generously shared your knowledges, your stories, and experiences to bring this book to life. As a most impressive group of Indigenous Early Career Researchers, it is wonderful to know the sector is in good hands and together we can disrupt Australian higher education and continue to build on the legacy of the many Indigenous people who have worked to make our universities places where Indigenous Australians can succeed and flourish.

Contents

Introduction: Retrofitting the Academy for Indigenous Excellence 1
Michelle Trudgett and Susan Page

Transitions and Expectations

Fate or Accident? A Story of Being in the Right Place, at the Right Time 15
Vinnitta Mosby

A Reflective Story of my Educational Learning Journey 21
Robyn Ober

A Letter to All the Deadly Accidental Academics Starting Their Early Career Researcher Journey 27
Katrina Thorpe

Navigation

Am I There Yet? Learning as I Go and Wondering What Success Looks Like 37
Michelle Locke

Musings About Work-Life Balance 45
Tracy Woodroffe

The Everyday of Risk and Vulnerability: Being an Indigenous Early Career Researcher 51
Vincent Backhaus

A Personal Story of 'Coincidence' in Becoming an Academic and Early Career Researcher: Being Creative to Push Boundaries 59
Anthony McKnight

Yuwa Indigenous Early Career Researcher 67
Skye Akbar

A Swim in the Rough Surf—Deaf, Aboriginal, and at the Biggest School of All 75
Scott Avery

Lessons Along the Way—8 Rules for Surviving Academia as an Aboriginal Early Career Researcher 81
BJ Newton

Aspirations

Mentoring Our Way for the Future of Indigenous Scholarship 91
Tristan Kennedy

Paving the Way from Latchkey Kid to Big Sky Dreaming 97
Corrinne T. Sullivan

Faith, Dreams and Lessons 103
Marcelle Townsend-Cross

Fishing Nets, River Banks and All the Things that Brought Me Here ... 109
Melinda Mann

Future Directions

Future Directions: Where the End is Actually the Beginning 117
Michelle Locke

Editors and Contributors

About the Editors

Professor Michelle Trudgett is an Indigenous scholar from the Wiradjuri Nation in New South Wales. Michelle currently holds the position of Deputy Vice-Chancellor Indigenous Leadership at Western Sydney University. She has also held senior positions at the University of Technology Sydney and Macquarie University. Michelle is currently the Chair of the Universities Australia Deputy/Pro Vice-Chancellor Indigenous Committee. She also serves as a Board Member on the GO Foundation. Michelle has received a number of awards including the highly prestigious National NAIDOC Scholar of the Year Award, the Neville Bonner Award for Teaching Excellence and the University of New England Distinguished Alumni Award.

Professor Susan Page is a national teaching award-winning Aboriginal educator and Indigenous higher education specialist, who is currently Pro Vice-Chancellor Indigenous Education at Western Sydney University. Susan's research focuses on Indigenous Australian experiences of learning and academic work in higher education and student learning in Indigenous Studies. She has collaborated on multiple competitive research grants and is well published in Indigenous Higher Education. Susan has held several leadership positions including Associate Dean (Indigenous Leadership and Engagement), Centre Director and Head of the Department and she is currently an appointed Indigenous representative for the Universities Australia Deputy Vice-Chancellor Academic committee.

Dr. Rhonda Povey is a non-Indigenous researcher, living and working on Dharug Country. She has extensive experience working and researching in the field of Indigenous education. Rhonda's place-based thesis, *The Proper Bad Lie: Aboriginal Responses to Western Education at Moola Bulla, 1910–1955*, focussed on rewriting colonial history of Aboriginal education in remote Australia was well received with a commendation for the Chancellor's award in 2020. She currently works at Western Sydney University in collaboration with Professors Trudgett, Professor Page and Dr. Locke on the *Developing Indigenous Early Career Researchers* project. The focus of Rhonda's doctoral thesis, current research and employment is working and standing with Indigenous peoples in advancing equity and parity in Indigenous education.

Dr. Michelle Locke is a Boorooberongal woman of the Dharug Nation, a very proud Mum of two boys and Western Sydney University alumnus. From January 2020 to December 2022 Michelle was employed firstly as a Professional Researcher and following the conferral of her Ph.D. in 2021 as a Postdoctoral Research Fellow with the Office of Deputy Vice-Chancellor Indigenous Leadership on the *Developing Indigenous Early Career Researchers* ARC project. In January 2023 Michelle commenced in the position of Senior Lecturer in the School of Education at Western Sydney University.

About the Contributors

Dr. Skye Akbar is a Waljen woman, a mum, sister and aunty. As a researcher and educator, her interests are Aboriginal business research, regional business research, research methods and ethics, community life, culturally informed local solutions and evidence-based decision-making.

Professor Scott Avery is an Indigenous researcher who is profoundly deaf. He developed his interest and approach to disability and inclusion research while working in community roles in the Australian Indigenous disability community, where he maintains a close connection with the First Peoples Disability Network. He has authored the book *Culture is Inclusion: A Narrative of Aboriginal and Torres Strait Islander Peoples with Disability* (2018) based on his research. He has extensive experience in conducting community-based research and policy in Indigenous and disability organisations and has been appointed as an expert advisor to numerous government bodies.

Dr. Vincent Backhaus completed his doctoral degree at The University of Cambridge, He matriculated from Trinity College, Cambridge in 2013. His graduate studies explored the connections between Traditional Knowledge and learning theory with a core focus on cognition and ways of teaching. He began postdoctoral work lecturing across the Indigenous Education and Research Centre (IERC) James Cook University, Indigenous studies undergraduate major, and continues to supervise students undertaking the JCU M.Phil., and the Ph.D. Indigenous HDR programme. Vincent is currently a Research Fellow at the Cairns Institute with co-investigators Associate Professor Felecia Watkin Lui and Professor Stewart Lockie working with Traditional Owners across the Great Barrier Reef to consider meaningful engagement with Great Barrier Reef Marine Park Authority and on water industry in the governance, care and management of Sea Country.

Professor Tristan Kennedy is a Noongar Aboriginal man, and a member of the Kaurna community in South Australia and the South-West Aboriginal Land and Sea Council in Western Australia. After five years working in the Department of Indigenous Studies at Macquarie University, he was recently appointed Professor and Pro Vice-Chancellor (Indigenous) at Monash University. Tristan has contemporary research interests, attracting growing international interest and collaboration in areas such as identities in online social spaces, Indigenous studies and education, and digital communication technologies.

Dr. Melinda Mann is a Darumbal and South Sea Islander woman, who lives and works on her homelands in Rockhampton, Queensland. She has over 25 years of experience in education and training. Melinda's scholarship draws from her professional experiences in school, tertiary and community education sectors; her lived experiences in regional and rural towns; and her commitment to nation building to assert First Nations sovereignty. She is a member of various advisory groups including a ministerial appointment to the Queensland Aboriginal and Torres Strait Islander Education and Training Committee.

Dr. Anthony McKnight is an Awabakal, Gumaroi and Yuin Man. Anthony is a father, husband, uncle, son, grandson, brother, cousin, nephew, friend and cultural man. Anthony is currently a Senior Lecturer in the School of Education, Faculty of the Arts, Social Sciences and Humanities. Anthony respects Country and values the knowledge that has been taught to him from Country, Elders and teachers from community(s). He continuously and respectfully incorporates Aboriginal ways of knowing and learning, with a particular interest of contributing to placing Country centre to validate Aboriginal approaches in academia and schools. In 2017, Anthony completed a Ph.D. called *Singing Up Country in Academia: Teacher education academics and preservice teachers' experience with Yuin Country*. He holds a Master of Education (HRD) from the University of Sydney and a Bachelor of Education, Health and Physical Education from the University of Wollongong.

Dr. Vinnitta Mosby is a Torres Strait Islander woman with family connections to the Murray Islands. Dr. Mosby was born and raised on Thursday Island, where she completed both primary and secondary education. After graduating with a Bachelor of Social Work (with first class honours), Dr. Mosby continued her studies with James Cook University, completing her Ph.D. in 2015. Since then, Dr. Mosby has been teaching in the School of Social Work and Human Services.

Dr. BJ Newton is a proud Wiradjuri woman and mother to three young children. BJ is a Senior Research Fellow at the Social Policy Research Centre within UNSW Sydney. She specialises in Indigenous research methods and child protection research and policy. Her research focuses on working in partnership with Aboriginal organisations to build evidence and support Aboriginal families interfacing with child protection systems. BJ was the inaugural Associate Dean (Indigenous) of the Faculty of Arts, Design and Architecture, a position which she held between January 2021 and August 2022. BJ then transitioned from this role to take up a prestigious Scientia Fellowship which enables her to focus on research.

Dr. Robyn Ober is a Mamu/Djirribal woman from Far North Queensland and a Lead Researcher at Batchelor Institute, Northern Territory. Her association with Batchelor Institute spans three decades. Robyn has been at the front line of the development of both ways of pedagogy, working to combine Indigenous and non-Indigenous ways of knowing, being and learning in teaching practice and in research. She has gathered awards for her teaching in Indigenous and both-ways higher education and vocational education training. Dr. Ober is a respected researcher in Indigenous educational leadership and both-ways teaching and learning, with her work appearing in conferences, journals and national reports. In her doctoral work, she investigated identity and culture expressed in and through Aboriginal English. Dr. Ober's expertise has been called upon in numerous consultancies on education delivery, both-ways education, Indigenous research methodologies in the Northern Territory, national and international Indigenous educational contexts.

Professor Corrinne Sullivan is an Aboriginal scholar from the Wiradjuri Nation in Central-West New South Wales. Her research interests are multi-disciplinary and focus broadly on experiences and effects of body and identity in relation to Aboriginal and Torres Strait Islander peoples. Corrinne's Honour's thesis entitled, 'Moral Linen: Indigenous and non-Indigenous experiences of dress in Parramatta Girls Home' was awarded the University Medal in Human Geography (2012). Her doctoral research explored the lived experiences of Aboriginal sex workers, Corrinne's thesis 'Indigenous Australian experiences of sex work: Stories of Agency, Autonomy and Self-Determination' was awarded the Vice-Chancellor's Commendation for Academic Excellence (2020). Corrinne's current work includes Indigenous and non-Indigenous experiences of sexuality and gender diversity through the perspectives of youth, older people, and sex workers.

Associate Professor Katrina Thorpe (Worimi) is the inaugural Chancellor's Postdoctoral Indigenous Research Fellow at the Centre for the Advancement of Indigenous Knowledges, University of Technology Sydney. Katrina has 25 years' of experience teaching mandatory Indigenous Studies within the fields of education, social work, nursing, health and community development. Drawing on these diverse teaching experiences, Katrina's research has engaged the voices of Aboriginal community members, pre-service teachers and teacher educators to provide deeper understandings of the experiences that support or inhibit student learning and development of a personal and professional commitment to Indigenous education.

Dr. Marcelle Townsend-Cross is a mixed heritage First Nations woman of Biripi, Worimi and Irish descent. Marcelle is an educator and researcher who currently teaches Aboriginal Studies at the University Centre for Rural Health for the University of Sydney. For over twenty years she has worked in higher education developing and delivering Indigenous Australian Studies subjects and degree courses at various universities. Marcelle holds a Ph.D. (2018) and a Master of Education (2009) from the University of Technology Sydney. Marcelle's Indigenous Australian heritage inspires her dual research focus on the history and contemporary manifestations and impacts of colonialism in Australia and on teaching and learning for social justice and social change.

Dr. Tracy Woodroffe is a Senior Lecturer and Coordinator in the Faculty of Arts and Society specialising in Education, Teaching Indigenous Learners and Indigenous Knowledge in Education. She is a local Warumungu Luritja woman with extensive experience in Early Childhood, Primary, Secondary and Tertiary classrooms. Dr. Woodroffe is interested in educational pedagogy, identity, perspective, and the use of Indigenous Knowledge in educational contexts. Her work includes Indigenous methodology through an Indigenous Women's Standpoint, and the use of Presentation Feedback.

Contributors

Dr. Skye Akbar University of South Australia, Adelaide, Australia

Professor Scott Avery University of Technology Sydney, Sydney, NSW, Australia

Dr. Vincent Backhaus The Cairns Institute, Nguma Bada Campus, James Cook University, Smithfield, Cairns, QLD, Australia

Professor Tristan Kennedy Monash University, Clayton, VIC, Australia

Dr. Michelle Locke Western Sydney University, Kingswood, NSW, Australia

Dr. Melinda Mann Central Queensland University, Rockhampton, Queensland, Australia

Dr. Anthony McKnight University of Wollongong, Wollongong, NSW, Australia

Dr. Vinnitta Mosby James Cook University, Cairns, Queensland, Australia

Dr. BJ Newton UNSW Sydney, Sydney, NSW, Australia

Dr. Robyn Ober Batchelor Institute of Indigenous Tertiary Education, Casuarina, NT, Australia

Professor Susan Page Western Sydney University, Parramatta, NSW, Australia

Professor Corrinne T. Sullivan Geography and Urban Studies, School of Social Sciences, Western Sydney University, Parramatta, NSW, Australia

Associate Professor Katrina Thorpe Nura Gili: Centre for Indigenous Programs, UNSW Sydney, Sydney, NSW, Australia

Dr. Marcelle Townsend-Cross University of Sydney, Sydney, NSW, Australia

Professor Michelle Trudgett Western Sydney University, Parramatta, NSW, Australia

Dr. Tracy Woodroffe Charles Darwin University, Casuarina, NT, Australia

Introduction: Retrofitting the Academy for Indigenous Excellence

Michelle Trudgett and Susan Page

1 Introduction

In this chapter, we discuss the marginalisation of Indigenous Australians in the higher education sector from the period when universities were first established through to more recent times. As you read, we ask you to not only consider the formation of the academy in which Indigenous scholars now work, but also how we continue to practice advocacy and self-determination in our research, teaching and engagement. It is important to have this background knowledge to appreciate the immense commitments and brave work undertaken by the pioneers of Indigenous education. Without their significant contributions to the sector, many of the chapters to follow this one would not be possible as they have paved the way for others to follow. While much has changed from the early days of marginalisation and low expectation, there remains work to be done to ensure that universities are genuine places of equal opportunity for Indigenous peoples. It is within this environment that Indigenous ECRs seek to build on their hard-won doctoral success.

2 Indigenous Higher Education in Australia

The Australian higher education system officially commenced with the establishment of the University of Sydney in 1850, followed by the University of Melbourne in 1853 (Horne & Sherington, 2010). By the time these universities were established

M. Trudgett (✉) · S. Page
Division of the Deputy Vice-Chancellor Indigenous Leadership, Western Sydney University, Parramatta, NSW, Australia
e-mail: michelle.trudgett@westernsydney.edu.au

S. Page
e-mail: s.page@westernsydney.edu.au

© The Author(s) 2025
M. Trudgett et al. (eds.), *Indigenous Early Career Researchers in Australian Universities*, SpringerBriefs in Education,
https://doi.org/10.1007/978-981-97-2823-7_1

in the mid-nineteenth century, colonisation was proceeding apace and Aboriginal peoples were already experiencing a decline in population due to introduced disease and frontier violence (Ryan, 2010). New waves of immigrants began arriving with the discovery of gold from the 1850s, increasing pressure on land and resources as the pastoral frontier was extending steadily out from the east coast. The two initial universities were followed by the formation of several other institutions around Australia—the University of Adelaide in 1874; the University of Tasmania in 1890; the University of Queensland in 1909; and University of Western Australia in 1911 (Partridge, 1965). Notably, all six states had a university by 1911, however only 3000 students were enrolled nation-wide. The University of Sydney and University of Melbourne housed two-thirds of all students enrolled in Australian universities in 1911 (Forsyth, 2015). Simultaneously, the dispossession of Aboriginal peoples from their traditional lands progressed unabated as the voracious colonial appetite for land grew, with many moved onto reserves overseen by government officials or missions run by religious organisations. Aboriginal peoples were also drawn (lured) into the pastoral industry as an unpaid labour force (Anthony, 2014).

It is clear from all reports that the original architects of Australia's higher education system were not experienced in designing a suite of institutions to meet the tertiary needs of a nation. In fact, they were very much novices who were catering for the elite. Some scholars such as Forsyth (2015) view this inexperience as a positive attribute as they were not attempting to replicate the design of another country's sector. However, other scholars such as Ma Rhea and Russell (2012) point to the fact that the original architects were drawing inspiration from the 'intellectual constructs of the British homelands' (p. 18). It is here that we need to pause to consider the significant disregard for Indigenous Australians to be included in the colonisers' education system. It is particularly important to acknowledge that colonialism and the elements it brings with it extend beyond just occupying land, as people's minds are also susceptible to being colonised (Nandy, 1983). The quest to psychologically occupy Indigenous minds was arguably one of the key tenets of the colonisers' strategic plan. Yet, this was done without exposure or opportunity to participate in the colony's education system.

A university education was afforded to those who had completed secondary schooling and could afford associated costs attributed to undertaking a university education—hence limited to the wealthy families (Tully & Whitehead, 2009). Whilst perhaps not the main reason underpinning the establishment of higher education in Australia, it became a vehicle to displace, disenfranchise, and disempower Indigenous peoples. In doing so, it reinforced a system where we became 'the Other' (Said, 1978) and the colonisers, particularly those with significant financial capacities, had positions of privilege and opportunity through such access to attain formal higher education qualifications.

3 Colonial (Mis)conceptions of Indigenous Ability

In Australia, Indigenous education has been influenced by an entrenched colonial notion of White superiority and Indigenous inferiority (Moreton-Robinson, 2005). The colonisers' initial assessment was that Indigenous people were savages who required conversion to Christianity to become civilised (Burridge & Chodkiewicz, 2012). Yet, in pre-colonial times, experiential and immersive forms of education enriched Indigenous children and young people with knowledge and skills to survive and flourish in their environments. Mission schools, often run by religious orders taking the opportunity to inculcate Western values and gender roles (Jensz, 2012) and recruit new converts, were early colonial attempts to disrupt Indigenous education as it had been practised for millennia. In the second half of the 1800s there was limited access to government schools (Burridge & Chodkiewicz, 2012). The emphasis, however, was on training Indigenous children for domestic or pastoral work, and absorption into White society's lower ranks (Reynolds, 2009).

Compulsory schooling for Aboriginal children up to the age of 12 was introduced in the late 1800s, although, those children could be removed from school if White parents made such a request (Reynolds, 2009). The subsequent exclusions contributed to a growing number of unschooled Aboriginal children creating a problem for governments of the time. Solutions to this problem included the development of widespread government powers to remove Aboriginal children from their families in the interests of child welfare. The child removals would culminate in the disastrous intergenerational trauma that is now well documented as the Stolen Generation (Barta, 2008; Read, 1998); moreover, the educative value of such removal is dubious. Povey (2020) for example, details the experiences of stolen children, and the deception of Aboriginal families who were promised a Western education for their children at Moola Bulla station in Western Australia. The children were largely used as unpaid labour rather than receiving an education. The expectation was that the children were incapable of higher learning. Torres Strait Islander scholar Nakata (2007) indicates:

> Up until the 1950s it was not uncommon to express the position that Australia's Indigenous people reached a point of intellectual development around adolescence where they could progress no more (p. 155).

These ideas of inferiority, and the low expectations of Indigenous peoples by successive governments, ensured that Indigenous Australians did not come to tertiary education until well into the twentieth century.

4 Indigenous Participation in the Academy

Despite the first university in Australia being established in 1850, it wasn't until the 1960s that the grand doors of these now well-established institutions opened to provide Indigenous Australians an opportunity to enrol in what was then deemed a

'Western education.' We must however be cognisant that if we continue to refer to universities as 'Western institutions' and the education programs on offer by these institutions as 'Western education' then we are deliberately choosing to marginalise ourselves in the narrative. It is important that we stop using this term and instead refer to universities as Global Institutions. Words have significant power, and we must ensure that the language we consciously use positions Indigenous peoples at the centre of the narrative and no longer on the margins.

There are a handful of Indigenous Australians who led the way in higher education to become pioneers at a time when institutional and systemic racism were rampant in institutions and the nation more broadly. These people must be acknowledged for their ability to succeed under such challenging times as they have led the way for others to follow. The first Indigenous person to receive a tertiary qualification is believed to be Dr Margo Weir who was awarded a Diploma of Physical Education from Melbourne University in 1959 (Cleverley & Mooney, 2010)—more than a century after they opened their doors. In 1966 Margaret Valadian would become the first Indigenous person to earn a Bachelor Degree graduating with a Bachelor of Social Studies from the University of Queensland. At the postgraduate level, the first known Indigenous person to receive a doctoral qualification was Dr Jonas who was awarded a PhD in 1980 from the University of Papua New Guinea (Bock, 2014).

Eckermann (1998) correctly states that 'any analysis of Aboriginal education clearly shows that it was marred by neglect until the 1970s' (p. 304). In the early 1970s there were fewer than one hundred Indigenous people enrolled in universities throughout Australia (Gale, 1998). Many people across the nation were misinformed and held the belief equality in higher education would be accomplished by 'adding Indigenous peoples to the academy of science and giving it a stir' (Rigney, 2001, p. 1).

Whilst this small cohort faced many obstacles, particularly given the new terrain they were navigating, one of the most glaring challenges was the realisation that they would most often not be taught by another Indigenous person as we were yet to build capacity in this space. Rather, these pioneers were predominantly reliant on non-Indigenous people to teach as there was only 18 Indigenous people employed in the sector in the early 1970s (Bin-Sallik, 2003)—this included the teaching of disciplines that included Indigenous content. Of note, was the formidable MaryAnn Bin-Sallik who was the first known Indigenous Australian to work in the higher education sector. Born in 1940, Emeritus Professor Bin-Sallik would go on to lead a most illustrious career contributing to the sector for several decades. On a personal note, she would even become a mentor to the first author of this chapter (Trudgett), which flourished into a lovely friendship.

The sector has seen Indigenous people cement their place as not just academics in the academy, but as incredibly powerful scholars with outstanding academic track records. There are now a collective group of leading Indigenous scholars who are often positioned as the 'Indigenous academic superstars'. Over time, they have left a valuable legacy of scholarship which not only speaks to their relevant academic disciplines, but also to their experiences within the academy. Their contributions have a permanent place in history as providing significant scholarly foundations for others.

Introduction: Retrofitting the Academy for Indigenous Excellence

We are no longer in a position where we are solely drawing on the academic theories of non-Indigenous scholars—instead we are creating our own theories. Today's ECRs enter a national and institution context that has been considerably changed by the work of these pioneers, both the well-known scholars and those academic and professional staff who have worked, with quiet determination, to Indigenise the academy. However, this progress has not been cost neutral—it has come with a physical, mental and emotional cost to many. Moreover, Indigenous people have, too often, been silenced by disciplinary training and marginalised within hierarchical structures, which at one time seemed impenetrable.

Professor Bronwyn Fredericks made the following statement in 2007—five years before she became the first Indigenous female to hold a Pro Vice-Chancellor Indigenous position:

> I have felt what it is like to be silenced. I have seen Aboriginal peoples left as the shadows of the speakers, as the speechless, the voiceless and the voice of absence. In this process we become re-written. We remain in the periphery and once again in the margin. We are again portrayed as 'object', and those who do the talking, the speaking about us, are again given the 'legitimacy' and further 'authority' to keep doing it, to keep making us 'voiceless objects'. These people are the 'cultural overseers' and the 'privileged interpreters' of Aboriginal peoples, issues and objects. In this, the places and spaces within higher education that used to speak about us become further sites of appropriation and objectification and not sites of emancipation, liberation, subjectivity, resistance and sites where we can individually and jointly speak. In making us speechless, voiceless and marginal and maintaining cultural overseer positions, possible sites of radical openness and challenge are lost (Fredericks, 2007, p. 17).

Drawing on this statement provided by Fredericks, we argue that there is a clear continuation of behaviour where people and systems have attempted to render the Indigenous voice as silent from the moment institutions were established through to more recent times. However, there is also very visible evidence that Indigenous resistance and extraordinary intellectual scholarship has successfully plied the doors of the academy open for others to follow.

5 Decades of Changes and Challenges

The chance to reflect on Indigenous participation in the sector has been one we welcome, particularly as it has provided us with an opportunity to reflect on the key changes and challenges during our time employed in it. We both identify as Indigenous women who have had a formal research partnership since 2011. Together, we offer 43 years of experience working in the academy and have seen many changes over time—the highs and lows have been constant. We have seen the environment shift from a time when the most senior Indigenous positions were housed in the Indigenous Student Centres designed to provide academic, cultural, and pastoral support to students. During the 1980s, 1990s and early 2000s these roles tended to be highly sought-after despite the reality that the responsibilities were immense but the resources available were minimal (Trudgett et al., 2022). Whilst these Centres still exist and continue to play an important role in Indigenous education across Australian universities, they are no longer the pinnacle position for the most senior Indigenous scholars.

In 2009 the Indigenous leadership landscape was positively disrupted by the introduction of a Pro Vice-Chancellor Indigenous appointment at Charles Darwin University. The University of Sydney took this one step further in 2011 and incorporated a Deputy Vice-Chancellor Indigenous Strategy and Services position into their senior leadership team. However, other universities did not demonstrate the same level of recognition and commitment to Indigenous leadership for quite some time, perhaps not realising the significant work undertaken by Indigenous leaders nor the benefits this can bring to an institution. It was not until August 2021 that Western Sydney University incorporated the second Deputy Vice-Chancellor Indigenous position (held by the first author of this chapter). Interestingly, other institutions then quickly followed this lead with Charles Darwin University introducing a Deputy Vice-Chancellor Indigenous position in October 2021 and James Cook University in November 2021; other institutions have also introduced similar positions in 2022 and 2023.

As we reflect on our time in the sector, we can see significant shifts in how Indigenous leaders have been incorporated into the governance structures of universities. It is clear that the sector has changed over time which is evidenced in the culmination of a number of factors including significant sector reviews such as the *Bradley Review of Australian higher education* (2008) and the *Behrendt Review of higher education outcomes for Aboriginal and Torres Strait Islander People* (2012); growth in Indigenous student numbers; an increase in Indigenous staff working in higher education; stronger policy implications—particularly through the key Commonwealth funding body the National Indigenous Australians Agency; and bolder strategic commitments within universities and across the sector through peak bodies such as Universities Australia.

While positive shifts are evident and it is clear we are making steady progress across many fronts, we must not become complacent nor rest on our laurels. There is much more work to be done to best serve the future generations of Indigenous peoples. For example, we have not reached student or staff parity and unfortunately remain under-represented in higher education. We are also yet to see an Indigenous Vice-Chancellor, though given the standing of the prominent Indigenous leaders currently holding Deputy Vice-Chancellor positions at the moment we do hold a newfound hope that this will not be far away.

6 A New Century Unfolds

In mid-2021 the Australian Bureau of Statistics released census data which indicated that Indigenous peoples represented 3.8% of the Australian population (Australian Bureau of Statistics, 2021). Population parity is a common benchmark used in education to assess Indigenous success. Yet, the latest Government statistical data available indicates that in 2020, there were 22,935 Indigenous students enrolled in a university qualification, equating to 2% of all domestic students (Department of Education, 2022). Notably, 586 of this cohort were enrolled in a doctoral degree. This is a strong increase on the figures presented earlier in this chapter which indicated that fifty years prior, there were less than 100 students enrolled across all levels of study in Australian universities. However, it is imperative to note that this number needs to be doubled to achieve population parity. It is also important to point out that in 2020, a total of 50 Indigenous people completed their doctoral qualification (Department of Education, 2022). The pipeline is growing, albeit slowly. The opportunities this growing cohort of Indigenous scholars represent is threefold. First as a potential workforce, second through contributing their Indigenous knowledge to research, teaching and institutional practice (Locke et al., 2022), and finally as role models for the next generation of Indigenous students studying at university.

Shifting our focus from students to staff, in 2021 there were 121,364 were employed in the Australian higher education sector of which 1691 (1.4%) identified as Indigenous Australian (Department of Education, 2022). Despite there now being a body of Indigenous people with academic qualifications, parity remains an aspiration rather than an actualisation. Sadly, encouraging Australian universities to employ more Indigenous people tends to fall in the remit of senior Indigenous staff as opposed to the Human Resources Departments or individual Schools/Faculties. In order to better serve our communities, all staff with leadership roles must actively commit to employing more Indigenous staff—this is imperative if we are truly going to progress the work of our universities.

7 Pivotal Moments of Change

There are undoubtedly many pivotal moments which have led to the current state of Indigenous education in Australia. Despite the challenges already noted, several critical events have led to growth across the sector in Indigenous students and staff, and to the appointment of senior Indigenous staff who contest Indigenous matters at some of the highest echelons of our universities, creating refashioned spaces for Indigenous people in higher education. Here we outline two key events which mark out periods that provided blueprints for the future. The first initiative, the commencement in 1990 of the National Aboriginal Education Policy, would set a standard for Indigenous education that has yet to be reached (Day et al., 2015). The second event, the launch of the first Universities Australia Indigenous Strategy, more than two decades later, catalysed a surge in Indigenous activity in universities.

More than a decade before the launch of the National Aboriginal Education Policy, the all-Indigenous National Aboriginal Education Committee (NAEC) had urged the government to fund centres to support Indigenous students in universities, to bolster the 1000 Indigenous Teachers initiative (Holt, 2020). Members of the NAEC understood that this anticipated significant wave of Indigenous students would need additional support to be successful in the university environments where they would be a small minority in the overall cohort (Holt & Morgan, 2016). Such centres were established and became the building blocks for renewed Indigenous achievement in higher education, championing institutional reform in teaching and research, fostering student growth, and producing the next generation of leaders (Page et al., 2017). The work of the Indigenous centres was often achieved with inadequate resources, and in university environments that were sometimes supportive and sometimes hostile. Many current Indigenous leaders in higher education have worked in these Indigenous Centres. More recently the original centres have from having a singular focus on supporting students to undertaking teaching and research and a range of Indigenous research centres have been established.

In March 2017, the peak body for Australian universities, Universities Australia, launched their first Indigenous Strategy (Universities Australia, 2017). The *Indigenous Strategy 2017–2020* was developed in collaboration with the National Aboriginal and Torres Straits Islander Higher Education Consortium (Aboriginal Corporation) and marked a clear shift in focus in relation to Indigenous higher education. The strategy outlined a national commitment to achieving better Indigenous outcomes in key areas of higher education such as student success, curriculum, and workforce. Research, and the bolstering of skilled capacity, positioned Indigenous ECRs as a central part of future workforce development.

Few pivotal moments occur in isolation. The Universities Australia Indigenous Strategy 2017–2020 was preceded by a number of key reviews and reports in the higher education sector. The *Review of Higher Education* (2008), the *National Best Practice Framework for Indigenous Cultural Competency in Australian Universities* (Universities Australia, 2011), the *National Indigenous Higher Education Workforce Strategy* (IHEAC, 2011) and the *Review of Higher Education Access and Outcomes for Aboriginal and Torres Strait Islander People* (Behrendt et al., 2012): all addressed aspects of Indigenous experience in the tertiary sector and drew national attention to Indigenous higher education. In turn, the Behrendt Review, for example, can be traced to Recommendation 30 of the *Review of Australian Higher Education*:

> That the Australian Government regularly review the effectiveness of measures to improve higher education access and outcomes for Indigenous people in consultation with the Indigenous Higher Education Advisory Council (Bradley et al., 2008, p. xxiii).

Amongst a plethora of recommendations from the Behrendt Review, aimed at accelerating Indigenous success outcomes in Australian higher education, a small cluster were directed to Early Career Researchers. The two major research funding agencies, the Australian Research Council and the National Health and Medical Research Council were encouraged to investigate barriers to Indigenous Australians winning competitive research funds and to explore ways to enhance the support for Indigenous ECRs in particular (Behrendt et al., 2012, p. xxiii). The authors of the review also urged universities to ensure that Indigenous doctoral and ECRs had access to high-quality training and research facilities and opportunities to undertake research (p. 117). In the decade since the Behrendt Review, Indigenous HDR student enrolments and completions have grown slowly, rising from 393 enrolments (Masters by Research and doctoral degrees) to 751 enrolments in 2020 (Universities Australia,

2022). The candidates successfully navigating this system are the Indigenous ECRs who will help to build the future of Indigenous research and success in Australian universities and perhaps beyond.

8 Brave New Voices—A New Direction

There is a great deal of work ahead of us if we, as a national sector, are to appropriately acknowledge the valuable contributions that Indigenous scholars bring to their profession. There is also much to be excited about in terms of the energy, enthusiasm and knowledge that the next generation of Indigenous researchers bring with them. In some respects, it would be reasonable to assert that we are retrofitting or redesigning the structures of the sector so that it can be the best it can be—for all of society. The sector has ethical and social responsibilities to the communities in which it serves as well as the nation more broadly and must be accountable for its actions and outcomes.

However Indigenous peoples cannot do this alone, and nor should we have to. Good allies are an important part of this process as we have spent considerable time building strong relationships with colleagues throughout the sector. We have invested in and remain committed to a collegial and joint narrative that positions Indigenous peoples at the centre of the conversation and not on the margins. We need to create spaces and opportunities that will consciously upset and disrupt the sector. As a collective, we need to see more conversations where it is no longer Indigenous people advocating for change for our people—but rather one where we have strong allies who willingly pick up a considerable component of this work which can be both emotionally, psychologically, and physically taxing—and in acknowledging this toll we need to actively support one another. The time where we view Indigenous education as something that has been relegated to the corner of universities for Indigenous staff to 'deal with' is no longer. Today, we ask the senior leadership to take a prominent role in creating opportunities for Indigenous peoples to both shine and thrive in a sector that is respectful and inclusive of our ways of knowing, being and doing.

This chapter precedes a series of contributions by Indigenous ECRs. It is their voices, experiences, ambitions and work that will direct and guide the sector so that it effectively serves and nurtures the next generation of scholars. They are clever, fierce and determined intellects who are each proud of their culture. Universities need these qualities in their leaders to be truly successful. Afterall, the voice of the first Indigenous Vice-Chancellor may well be in one of these chapters.

References

Anthony, T. (2014). Indigenous stolen wages: Historical exploitation and contemporary injustice. *Precedent, 118*, 42–46.

Australian Bureau of Statistics. (2021). *Estimates of Aboriginal and Torres Strait Islander Australians.* https://www.abs.gov.au/statistics/people/aboriginal-and-torres-strait-islander-peoples/estimates-aboriginal-and-torres-strait-islander-australians/jun-2021#age-and-sex-structure

Barta, T. (2008). Sorry, and not sorry, in Australia: How the apology to the stolen generations buried a history of genocide. *Journal of Genocide Research, 10*(2), 201–214. https://doi.org/10.1080/14623520802065438

Behrendt, L., Larkin, S., Griew, R., & Kelly, P. (2012). *Review of higher education outcomes for Aboriginal and Torres Strait Islander People.* Commonwealth of Australia.

Bin-Sallik, M. A. (2003). Cultural safety: Let's name it! *The Australian Journal of Indigenous Education, 32*(1), 21–28.

Bock, A. (2014, March 17). Academics open doors to social benefits. *The Age-Education Supplement* (p. 14).

Bradley, D., Noonan, P., Nugent, H., & Scales, B. (2008). *Review of Australian higher education. Final report.* http://hdl.voced.edu.au/10707/44384

Burridge, N., & Chodkiewicz, A. (2012). An historical overview of Aboriginal education policies in the Australian context. In N. Burridge, F. Whalan, & K. Vaughn (Eds.), *Indigenous education: A learning journey for teachers, schools and communities* (pp. 11–22). Sense Publishers. https://doi.org/10.1007/978-94-6091-888-9

Cleverley, J., & Mooney, J. (2010). *Taking our place: Aboriginal education and the story of the Koori Centre at the University of Sydney* (pp. 27–28). Sydney University Press.

Day, A., Nakata, V., Nakata, M., & Martin, G. (2015). Indigenous students' persistence in higher education in Australia: Contextualising models of change from psychology to understand and aid students' practices at a cultural interface. *Higher Education Research & Development, 34*(3), 501–512.

Department of Education. (2022). *Higher education statistics.* https://www.education.gov.au/higher-education-statistics

Eckermann, A.-K. (1998). The economics of Aboriginal education. *International Journal of Social Economics, 25*(2/3/4), 302–313.

Forsyth, H. (2015). *A history of the Modern Australian University.* University of New South Wales Publishing.

Fredericks, B. (2007). Utilising the concept of pathways as a framework for indigenous research. *Australian Journal of Indigenous Education, 36*(S), 15–22.

Gale, P. (1998). *Indigenous rights and tertiary education in Australia.* Paper presented at the Annual Conference of the Australian Association for Research in Education (Adelaide, Australia, November 29–December 3).

Holt, L. (2020). Indigenous higher education in historical context in Australia. In P. Anderson, K. Maeda, Z. M. Diamond, & C. Sato (Eds.), *Post-imperial perspectives on indigenous education* (pp. 91–110). Routledge.

Holt, L., & Morgan, R. (2016). Empowering Aboriginal aspirations in Australian university structures and systems. *Higher Education Research and Development, 39*, 96–105.

Horne, J., & Sherington, G. (2010). Extending the educational franchise: The social contract of Australia's public universities, 1850–1890. *Paedagogica Historica, 46*(1–2), 207–227. https://doi.org/10.1080/00309230903528637

Indigenous Higher Education Advisory Council. (2011). *National Indigenous higher education workforce strategy: Indigenous Higher Education Advisory Council.* http://www.deewr.gov.au/Indigenous/HigherEducation/Programs/IHEAC/Documents/NIHEWS.pdf

Jensz, F. (2012). Missionaries and indigenous education in the 19th-century British Empire. Part I: Church-state relations and indigenous actions and reactions. *History Compass, 10*(4), 294–305.

Locke, M., Trudgett, M., & Page, S. (2022). Beyond the doctorate: Exploring Indigenous early career research trajectories. *The Australian Journal of Indigenous Education, 51*(1). https://ajie.atsis.uq.edu.au/ajie/issue/current

Ma Rhea, Z., & Russell, L. (2012). The invisible hand of pedagogy in Australian indigenous studies and indigenous education. *Australian Journal of Indigenous Education, 41*(1), 18–25. https://doi.org/10.1017/jie.2012.4

Moreton-Robinson, A. (2005). The house that Jack built: Britishness and white possession. *Australian Critical Race and Whiteness Studies Association Journal, 1*, 21–29.

Nakata, M. (2007). The cultural interface. *The Australian Journal of Indigenous Education, 36*(5), 2–14.

Nandy, A. (1983). *The intimate enemy: Loss and recover of self under colonialism*. Oxford University Press.

Page, S., Trudgett, M., & Sullivan, C. (2017). Past, present and future: Acknowledging indigenous achievement and aspiration in higher education. *HERDSA Review of Higher Education, 4*, 29–51.

Partridge, P. H. (1965). Universities in Australia. *Comparative Education, 2*(1), 19–30. https://doi.org/10.1080/0305006650020103

Povey, R. G. (2020). *The proper-bad lie: Aboriginal responses to western education at Moola Bulla, 1910–1955* (Unpublished doctoral dissertation). University of Technology Sydney.

Read, P. (1998). The return of the stolen generation. *Journal of Australian Studies, 22*(59), 8–19. https://doi.org/10.1080/14443059809387421

Reynolds, R. J. (2009). "Clean, clad and courteous" revisited: A review history of 200 years of Aboriginal education in New South Wales. *Journal of Negro Education, 78*(1), 83–94.

Rigney, L.-I. (2001). A first perspective of Indigenous Australian participation in science: Framing Indigenous research towards Indigenous Australian intellectual sovereignty. *Kaurna Higher Education, 7*, 1–13.

Ryan, L. (2010). Settler massacres on the Port Phillip frontier, 1836–1851. *Journal of Australian Studies, 34*(3), 257–273.

Said, E. (1978). *Orientalism*. Pantheon Books.

Trudgett, M., Page, S., & Coates, S. K. (2022). Great expectations: Senior indigenous leadership positions in higher education. *Journal of Higher Education Policy and Management, 44*(1), 90–106.

Universities Australia. (2011). *National Best Practice Framework for Indigenous Cultural Competency in Australian Universities October 2011*. https://universitiesaustralia.edu.au/wp-content/uploads/2019/06/National-Best-Practice-Framework-for-Indigenous-Cultural-Competency-in-Australian-Universities.pdf

Universities Australia. (2017). *Indigenous Strategy 2017–2020*. https://www.universitiesaustralia.edu.au/policy-submissions/diversityequity/universities-australias-indigenous-strategy-2017-2020/

Universities Australia. (2022). *Indigenous strategy annual report* (4th edn.). https://www.universitiesaustralia.edu.au/wp-content/uploads/2022/08/UA_Indigenous_Strategy_Annual_Report_May-2022.pdf

Whitehead, C., & Tully, K. (2009). Audacious beginnings: The establishment of universities in Australasia 1850–1900. *Education Research and Perspectives, 36*(2), 1–44.

Professor Michelle Trudgett is an Indigenous scholar from the Wiradjuri Nation in New South Wales. Michelle currently holds the position Deputy Vice-Chancellor Indigenous Leadership at Western Sydney University. She has also held senior positions at the University of Technology Sydney and Macquarie University. Michelle is currently the Chair of the Universities Australia Deputy/Pro Vice-Chancellor Indigenous Committee. She also serves as a Board Member on the GO Foundation. Michelle has received a number of awards including the highly prestigious National NAIDOC Scholar of the Year Award, the Neville Bonner Award for Teaching Excellence and the University of New England Distinguished Alumni Award.

Professor Susan Page is a national teaching award-winning Aboriginal educator and Indigenous higher education specialist, who is currently Pro Vice-Chancellor Indigenous Education at Western Sydney University. Susan's research focuses on Indigenous Australian experiences of learning and academic work in higher education and student learning in Indigenous Studies. She has collaborated on multiple competitive research grants and is well published in Indigenous Higher Education. Susan has held several leadership positions including Associate Dean (Indigenous Leadership and Engagement), Centre Director and Head of the Department and she is currently an appointed Indigenous representative for the Universities Australia Deputy Vice Chancellor Academic committee.

Open Access This chapter is licensed under the terms of the Creative Commons Attribution 4.0 International License (http://creativecommons.org/licenses/by/4.0/), which permits use, sharing, adaptation, distribution and reproduction in any medium or format, as long as you give appropriate credit to the original author(s) and the source, provide a link to the Creative Commons license and indicate if changes were made.

The images or other third party material in this chapter are included in the chapter's Creative Commons license, unless indicated otherwise in a credit line to the material. If material is not included in the chapter's Creative Commons license and your intended use is not permitted by statutory regulation or exceeds the permitted use, you will need to obtain permission directly from the copyright holder.

Transitions and Expectations

Fate or Accident? A Story of Being in the Right Place, at the Right Time

Vinnitta Mosby

Undertaking tertiary studies is often a privilege, although it can come with many struggles, especially for self-funded mature aged students who frequently have to juggle family, work, and study. Completing an undergraduate degree can seem like a tough slog, especially when studying part-time. To then consider adding an additional few extra year to do a Ph.D. would seem excruciating. In this chapter, I share my story to encourage Indigenous tertiary graduates who are considering taking the Ph.D. route, as a continuation of their degrees or as returning students. I was an accidental Early Career Academic and Researcher. Although I had not intended to hang around after submitting my thesis, a position became vacant and I was encouraged to apply as there were no Aboriginal and/or Torres Strait Islander academics teaching in the social work degree. Initially, I was going to give it three years, get through probation and then get out. My heart was in back in the community and my sight was on returning home to the islands.

For the purpose of this chapter, I will start by introducing my cultural identity and background, then revisit the route taken, and reflect back on some of the challenges, opportunities and support experienced throughout my academic journey. My intention here is to inform, encourage and inspire others to anticipate, plan and navigate the journey ahead. I am using storytelling as a method to share knowledge as its congruent with Indigenous epistemologies and for me the most natural process that has a beginning, middle and an end.

I am a Torres Strait Islander woman with cultural ties to the Meriam Nation. My mother is from the *Komet* tribe, whose culture and traditions I inherit. I take my totem the sea turtle (*Nam*) from my grandmother. *Nam* is renowned for travelling alone over great distances, but no matter how far she travels, she always returns to nest in the sands of her origins. Likewise, I must return home no matter how far I

V. Mosby (✉)
James Cook University, Cairns, Queensland, Australia
e-mail: vinnitta.mosby@jcu.edu.au

© The Author(s) 2025
M. Trudgett et al. (eds.), *Indigenous Early Career Researchers in Australian Universities*, SpringerBriefs in Education,
https://doi.org/10.1007/978-981-97-2823-7_2

venture. My children are many, and my lineage transcends several generations. The North Westerlies, *Koki*, is my totemic wind. I belong to the subgroup, *Sab Koki*. *Koki* arrives swiftly but briefly during the monsoon period of November and March, bringing much-needed rain after the long dry spell of the South Easterly, *Sager*. *Koki* cleanses the islands, replenishment vital water supplies and readies people for the new year. Introducing my cultural identity is important as this sets the platform from where I stand and from where I speak. I am a woman with ongoing connections to place but reside outside of the homelands and therefore reminded that I cannot speak for all Torres Strait Islanders or Meriam peoples per se. Acknowledging Country and custodians of the lands, sea and skies is important to Indigenous peoples as when I am away from home, I am a visitor on other people's Country. In doing so, I am respecting diversity and sovereignty within the larger Indigenous Nations to counter the homogenisation of Indigenous peoples.

I grew up on Thursday Island, the homelands of the Kaurareg Nation. In many ways, I was protected from the harsh realities faced by folks living on mainland Australia. Where services and opportunities were lacking on Thursday Island, a close-knit and nurturing community compensated by providing a conducive environment for children to grow and thrive. I now live in Cairns, on the lands of the Gimay-Wullaburra, Yidinji and Yirrganydji Nations. Nonetheless, Thursday Island is still considered home. I have been fortunate to return at least twice a year to catch up with family, attend cultural events and fulfil social obligations. I am a mother, a grandmother, and a Social Work Lecturer at James Cook University (JCU).

A career in academia was not the intention for completing a Ph.D., but rather a personal quest of exploration to find answers to long-held questions. I was concerned about climate change and what that might mean to Torres Strait Islanders, whose spirituality, value systems and worldviews are place-based,[1] if forced to move. I intended to undertake a Ph.D. in my later years, but by fate and of course hard work, the journey unraveled much earlier. Graduating with First Class Honours in Social Work in 2010, with an Academic Medal for Coursework, put me in good stead to apply for a scholarship, which I was fortunate to secure. Six months later I commenced my candidature with JCU. The Ph.D. was an extension of my honours thesis where I explored Torres Strait Islander spirituality outside of *place* (Mosby, 2010). I wanted to know how people understood spirituality and maintained connection when living away. The honours project revealed that Torres Strait Islander spirituality encompassed sea, sky, winds, and the natural environment. Sky includes stars and constellations conveyed in stories identified with particular clan groups and families. Similarly, winds have totemic significance to clan groups and tribes. You belong to the winds that blow in the direction of your tribal lands—belonging in the sense that you are a part of the elements, the changing seasons and the environment. There was also the need to recreate familiar spaces and senses in the new location, recreating the sounds, sights, smells, and feelings of home. The simple acts of raking leaves, making fire, and looking out over the ocean were subconscious grounding strategies that people used to reconnect, find peace, and regain purpose.

---

[1] The meaning of place is synonymous with the Aboriginal concept of Country.

In my doctoral research, I set out to explore Torres Strait Islanders' experiences of the contemporary out-migration of people who had moved to the mainland to understand how they were managing their experience of resettlement in Cairns. The study was inspired by my own experience of resettlement and the sense of displacement that lasted for some time after moving. I felt I had left my spirit behind on the islands and each time I returned home, I would leave feeling homesick. It took some years before I could unpack my life in Cairns. This feeling of temporary existence seemed to me like 'living out of a suitcase'. I wondered if other Torres Strait Islanders felt the same way and if so, how were they managing their experiences. Most importantly, I wanted to provide a reference for others by uncovering separate experiences of internal migration, especially with the threat of climate change and predicted forced migration. From this study, I found resettlement took time, people experienced being out of place, and they managed the experience of uncertainty and homesickness by keeping close to family and culture, maintaining purpose, and drawing on the hope of one day returning home to the islands (Mosby, 2015).

The question of how I got to be an Early Career Researcher often crosses my mind. Here I am, an island girl teaching social work to predominately Anglo-Australians and helping students unpack uncomfortable topics such as racism, discrimination, and White privilege. Looking back, I am reminded of how blessed I was to meet wonderful people throughout my journey, people who were genuinely interested in what I had to say: I was more than a figment of the past, some idealist notion of a civilised native. I had family still on the islands who made sure my children were taken care of during school holidays and that I had a place to return to and recuperate during semester breaks. Going home was grounding and provided downtime away from the busyness of life on the mainland. Most importantly, I had an amazing advisory team who kept me going throughout the three and a half years it took to complete the Ph.D.

I am also reminded of how lucky I was because choosing your advisory team is not always possible. Finding someone available, committed, personally compatible and competent in supervising the proposed research topic can be challenging. Fortunately, I knew both of my advisors, who were teaching and leading researchers in the same faculty I was enrolled in. My supervisors were not Indigenous. Professor Komla Tsey was Ghanian and had worked extensively within Indigenous research. Associate Professor Wendy Earles was an Anglo-Australian had supervised another Indigenous student who spoke highly of her as a supervisor. Moreover, face-to-face in person supervisions was for me non-negotiable. Both supervisors brought different perspectives and were removed enough from the research topic to allow me the freedom to explore, create and drive the research. In the second year just before data collection, I had the privilege of meeting Canadian First Nations academic Margaret Kovach who was visiting Cairns on her sabbatical. Margaret was able to breakdown for me what Indigenous Methodologies encompassed from her own research. Talking to Margaret really grounded my project and gave me the confidence to move forward, without fear of not being seen as doing 'proper' research in Western terms.

There was also no way that I was moving further south just to complete a Ph.D. For starters, I do not like to be cold, and I needed to be close to home. Kiley and

Austin (2008) found in their study of Australian postgraduate research candidates, that candidates chose to continue studying at their current universities rather than moving, despite the incentive of scholarships. They also found that the honours pathway was the most accessible means of gaining entry and scholarships. JCU offered embedded honours in the fourth year of the social work degree and was the path I took that led me into the Ph.D. I guess I was in the right place, with the right people, at the right time.

Studies have found that retention and timely completions hinge on developing good relationships between supervisors and students, along with setting clear milestones and expectations upfront, meeting regularly, and writing early (Kiley, 2011). Looking back, I am grateful to have advisors who were available and encouraged regular face-to-face meetings. Face-to-face contact is not always possible. Again, I was lucky. Fortnightly meetings kept me on track and forced me to write critically and organise my thoughts from day one. Feedback was received during supervision and new tasks would be set for the following fortnight. I would then send an email to the advisor with a summary of the tasks to ensure accountability on both parts. My primary advisor was highly organised and disciplined and, because of that, I was able to submit my thesis on time.

Receiving a scholarship was another key factor that made the Ph.D. experience manageable by alleviating the financial stress (Martinez et al., 2013). The scholarship meant that I did not have to work full-time, allowing for uninterrupted focus on the project which was necessary for facilitating the depth of work and commitment that was required. I supplemented the scholarship by tutoring Indigenous social work students at JCU. Besides providing additional income, tutoring kept afresh discipline knowledge. Maintaining peer contact was important as the Ph.D. journey can be lonely. It also provided a sense of solidarity, reminding me why I had become a social worker.

Having the freedom to choose a meaningful topic was another key ingredient that sustained me throughout. The journey was a time of deep reflection and self-discovery which frequently meant drifting off course. Trudgett's (2014) study on supervising Indigenous Australian doctoral candidates found that students need room to move, find their feet and explore, and to own their research. Once a safe environment is established, students are able to come back and ask questions of their research. Like me, the candidates in the study stated that they did not want to be micromanaged and provided prescriptions without room for negotiation. I needed time and freedom as I understood the world through the lens of a Torres Strait Islander woman whose understanding of the seen and unseen world is infused with colonisation, western sciences, and Christianity. Attempting to integrate new understandings also created conflicts within, raising more questions, disillusionment, and discomfort. The embodiment of this process, a lived experience, a feeling, was important to appreciate who I was and what I stood for. I was a product of the time and context in which I existed, and therefore needed to delve deep within my psyche to integrate (or not) other ways of thinking, knowing, and doing.

Undertaking a Ph.D. is a life-changing journey, a privilege, and a one-time opportunity to do what you want and need to do. I did not set out to become an academic, but by accident or by fate the opportunity presented. Several factors enriched my Ph.D. experience and supported me through life's challenges. The support of my family back on the islands and the new friendships I made in Cairns kept me going. Amazing Ph.D. advisors understood that at times I needed to attend to family matters, or simply retreat, explore, and recalibrate. Without the scholarship, I might have returned to the workforce churning away with no guarantee of taking up the Ph.D. in later years as I had intended. Most important, however, was being able to choose a research topic that was meaningful to me, whose future, culture, and identity are being threatened by climate change. I had the privilege of learning to live deeply, to walk intentionally by placing one foot in front of the other when navigating uncharted territories. I was encouraged to trust the process, to be open to new ways of being and to trust intuition.

By fate or accident, the Ph.D. journey opened doors to academia, a passage I had not envisioned or thought I would enjoy. I want to believe it is fate, because at this point in time, I feel I am in the right place.

References

Kiley, M. (2011). Developments in research supervisor training: Causes and responses. *Studies in Higher Education, 36*(5), 585–599. https://doi.org/10.1080/03075079.2011.594595

Kiley, M., & Austin, A. (2008). Australian postgraduate research students still prefer to 'stay at home': Reasons and implications. *Journal of Higher Education Policy and Management, 30*(4), 351–362. https://doi.org/10.1080/13600800802383026

Martinez, E., Ordu, C., Della Sala, M. R., & McFarlane, A. (2013). Striving to obtain a school-work-life balance: The full-time doctoral student. *International Journal of Doctoral Studies, 8*, 39–59. https://doi.org/10.28945/1765

Mosby, V. P. (2010). *Place your feet on the ground, look up, and connect with the winds: Torres Strait Islander understandings of spirituality and its links to place.* Townsville.

Mosby, V. P. (2015). *Torres Strait Islanders' experiences of contemporary out-movement: A grounded theory of 'Living in Two Worlds'* (Unpublished doctoral dissertation). James Cook University. https://researchonline.jcu.edu.au/42367/

Trudgett, M. (2014). Supervision provided to Indigenous Australian doctoral students: A black and white issue. *Higher Education Research & Development, 33*(5), 1035–1048. https://doi.org/10.1080/07294360.2014.890576

Dr. Vinnitta Mosby is a Torres Strait Islander woman with family connections to the Murray Islands. Dr. Mosby was born and raised on Thursday Island, where she completed both primary and secondary education. After graduating with a Bachelor of Social Work (with first class honours), Dr. Mosby continued her studies with James Cook University, completing her Ph.D. in 2015. Since then, Dr. Mosby has been teaching in the School of Social Work and Human Services.

Open Access This chapter is licensed under the terms of the Creative Commons Attribution 4.0 International License (http://creativecommons.org/licenses/by/4.0/), which permits use, sharing, adaptation, distribution and reproduction in any medium or format, as long as you give appropriate credit to the original author(s) and the source, provide a link to the Creative Commons license and indicate if changes were made.

The images or other third party material in this chapter are included in the chapter's Creative Commons license, unless indicated otherwise in a credit line to the material. If material is not included in the chapter's Creative Commons license and your intended use is not permitted by statutory regulation or exceeds the permitted use, you will need to obtain permission directly from the copyright holder.

A Reflective Story of my Educational Learning Journey

Robyn Ober

1 Introduction

My name and title is Dr. Robyn Ober and I am a proud Mamu/Djirribal woman from Far North Queensland and a lead researcher at Batchelor Institute, Northern Territory. My association with Batchelor Institute spans three decades where I have been at the front line of the development of both-ways pedagogy, which is an educational approach to combine Indigenous and non-Indigenous ways of knowing, being and learning in teaching practice and in research. I have received awards for teaching in Indigenous and both-ways higher education and vocational education training. I have gained recognition as a respected researcher in Indigenous educational leadership and both-ways teaching and learning, with my work appearing in conferences, journals, and national reports. In my doctoral work, I investigated identity and culture expressed in and through Aboriginal English. My expertise has been called upon in numerous consultancies on education delivery, both-ways education, Indigenous research methodologies in the Northern Territory, national and international Indigenous educational contexts.

2 My Educational Story—Significant Events

On reflection of my life's experiences, critical incidents highlight significant events that shifted the direction of my educational journey. In 1982 Batchelor College (previous name of Batchelor Institute) was introduced to me by my dear Aunty Madge who was passionate about Indigenous education and encouraged me to enrol

---

R. Ober (✉)
Batchelor Institute of Indigenous Tertiary Education, Casuarina, NT, Australia
e-mail: robyn.ober@batchelor.edu.au

© The Author(s) 2025
M. Trudgett et al. (eds.), *Indigenous Early Career Researchers in Australian Universities*, SpringerBriefs in Education,
https://doi.org/10.1007/978-981-97-2823-7_3

in the Associate Diploma of Teaching in Aboriginal Schools as she strongly believed that 'Aboriginal children need Aboriginal teachers'. Aunty Madge worked as a primary school teacher at Ludmilla School (Darwin) in the 1980s and had recently completed her teacher education studies at Batchelor College. I began my teacher education course at Batchelor Institute in Indigenous Tertiary Education (BIITE) in 1983 and graduated with the Bachelor of Arts in Education Degree through the D-BATE (Deakin- Batchelor Aboriginal Teacher Education) program in 1986. My first teaching post was at Gunbalunya (Oenpelli) school in Western Arnhem land, followed by Clyde Fenton School in Katherine and finally the 'Murri School' in inner city Brisbane. These teaching experiences completed a rich experience of teaching in a remote, rural and urban primary school contexts. These different contexts provided the professional experiences that prepared and equipped me to teach in tertiary educational contexts.

In 1991, I returned to Batchelor Institute as a tutor (Lecturer A) and worked in a team-teaching situation alongside non-Aboriginal and Aboriginal Lecturers. The delivery of curriculum content was structured into teaching blocks where students attended two-week workshops at Batchelor or Central Australia campus and then returned to their home communities to completed required assessment tasks. This way of studying looked very different to what I remembered in the 1980s, where we resided on campus for four years before our first teaching post, however there were also obvious advantages of studying through mixed-mode delivery, where students were community-based and highly engaged with key educational issues in their schools.

In 1994 I successfully applied for an academic Lecturer B position which involved curriculum development, planning, delivering and evaluating workshops. Workshops were help on-campus and off-campus depending on the student cohort, and their community obligations and situations. In 2007 I completed the Master's in Applied Linguistics through Charles Darwin University before transferring to the Research Division after teaching for 14 years in VET/Higher Education in Teacher Education at BIITE.

As an early researcher I was offered opportunities to work alongside experienced researchers who were involved in projects focusing on Indigenous educational leadership, both-ways education, and Indigenous languages and linguistics. I have gleaned new knowledge from my colleagues and research participants to enable me to draw on our Indigenous ways of doing research with our people from an authentic and genuine standpoint.

3 My Ph.D. Journey

I have been inspired by prominent Indigenous Australian academics who have paved the way for me to complete a Ph.D. At the Tiddas (sisters) workshop (2007–2009, Australian Catholic University and Flinders University) we celebrated those who had completed their Ph.D.s and recognised the determination of those who were nearing the completion of their Ph.D. These 'Tiddas' workshops were a turning point in my educational journey and were instrumental in pushing me towards enrolling in postgraduate studies. An opportunity came my way in 2012 when I was awarded an Indigenous Research Collaboration (IRC) Doctoral Fellowship at Batchelor Institute of Indigenous Tertiary Education along with three of my Indigenous colleagues, Kathryn Gilbey and Jeanie Bell. My Ph.D. research study focused on Aboriginal English as a social, cultural and identity marker in Indigenous Tertiary Education and the role language plays in making meaning and deeper understanding of new professional educational concepts through our home talk.

Aboriginal English is the lingua franca for the majority of Aboriginal Australians resulting from racist policies which prevented Indigenous people from speaking their traditional languages and dialects. The Aboriginal people, in their intellectual brilliance, took hold of the foreign, enforced English language and began to mould, shape and appropriate it, to make it their own and express their own Aboriginality. There is an unspoken assumption in the dominant society that, communicative capability in standard Australian English signifies a person of high intellectual ability which is far from the truth.

In a tertiary educational context, adult Indigenous students bring their own conceptual understandings that are rich and highly intellectual, however, it becomes difficult and frustrating when students attempt to communicate and capture that high level knowledge in a language that is not their own. There is a danger of losing the rich and intrinsic meaning of the intended message through a foreign language that fails to capture intrinsic details of complex cultural conceptual understandings.

Language, culture, and identity are tightly embedded and intertwined with each other. The purpose of my Ph.D. was to recognise that Indigenous adult students naturally draw on their social, cultural and linguistic repertoires to make meaning of and rigorously engage in new professional concepts in the teaching and learning space. This study involved collecting classroom discourse in teacher education workshops, identifying critical linguistic incidents with student and staff (Aboriginal and non-Aboriginal), transcribing, analysing and recording the findings/outcomes from the collected data.

Over the years I have learnt to draw on Indigenous ways of being, doing and knowing to enable me to carve out new ways of undertaking research with Indigenous people. These new ways of thinking about research led me to identify and develop the 'Kapati (cup of tea) methodology where participants were encouraged to share stories (individual and collective) around a Kapati just like we do at home. There is nothing special about the 'Kapati', rather it is recognising this social event as a trigger for Indigenous students to engage in storytelling that encompasses layers of rich stories within a both-ways educational environment. The stories were then collected and analysed to identify the critical moments where students engaged in expanding their knowledge base by drawing on their social, cultural and linguistic repertoires. I am constantly seeking ways to work in collaboration and network with Indigenous and non-Indigenous researchers within Australia and overseas. These studies have provided opportunities to publish research findings in national and international journals including book chapters. I have emerged and developed as an active researcher in Indigenous education for over 15 years and have strengthened my knowledge base in the research space, pushing the boundaries as to how research can evolve and be inclusive of Indigenous ways of knowing, being and doing.

The Ph.D. journey took seven years in total to complete, but finally in 2019 I received my Ph.D. entitled *'Aboriginal English as a Social, Cultural and Identity Marker in Indigenous Tertiary Education'* as Doctor of Philosophy – Indigenous Perspectives. The completion of my Ph.D. was total emotional relief as the Doctoral Award was presented to me on graduation day at Batchelor Institute in June 2019. In the days, weeks, and months ahead I actually felt a bit strange as my whole life revolved around the thesis and now that period was over, I was suddenly thrust into the next chapter of my life where there was a high demand on my time. Now in place of writing chapters and finalising the thesis, there were requests to publish journal articles and book chapters, sit on advisory committees, guest speak and teach in various forums, symposiums and conferences.

4 Moving Forward

Although these were great opportunities for further development and growth, I found I had to say 'no' to some requests to allow time to find my own routine and personal rest.

Since completion of my Ph.D., I have had several offers to participate in grants as a Chief Investigator or participant on a range of research projects, focusing on educational leadership, both-ways education, Indigenous knowledges, language and linguistics, and Indigenous education, not all of which I have been able to accept.

I also have a teaching load in higher education which meant through the Charles Darwin University (CDU) and BIITE current partnership I am responsible for planning and delivering higher education course programs to Indigenous students at Batchelor campus in Northern Territory and teaching CDU external and internal students through online platforms. At times the research and teaching load can become quite heavy, and it is easy to become overwhelmed while also dealing with family, community, and personal issues. In these situations, it is helpful to seek experienced mentors from senior academics who can offer advice and direction to ensure our mental state and well-being are intact and in good health. There are times when it is wise to say 'no' to requests from external agencies which are not part of your primary duties although it is also good to network and develop strong relationships in the research and academic space.

For our students to succeed in university studies, there is a need for support and encouragement from academics and staff members at all levels. We, as Aboriginal and non-Aboriginal staff members, have an important responsibility to see Indigenous students from entry to completion of course studies. It is a learning journey and there will be challenges, obstacles, barriers and struggles, but there will also be rewards, celebrations and achievements. It is important to keep the end destination in sight and not be tempted to detour or go 'off track', as we as support staff at all levels want to see our students succeed and complete to the end. In my own learning journey, my supervisors allowed me to journey on my own for a time to develop independence and resilience, but when they saw I was struggling, they were the first ones to appear by my side to encourage and cheer me on.

As an Indigenous educator and researcher, I have enjoyed working in collaboration with my colleagues, and people to encourage and support them. I aspire to inspire others by shining a light on their potentials and strengths while celebrating their short term and long-term achievements. Sometimes we can see strengths in others that may be invisible to them. Therefore, they need to be told, reminded, and celebrated. As an academic, lecturer and researcher, I do hold that position of influence and I do take that role seriously. Aboriginal and Torres Strait Islander peoples have the intellectual brilliance to run their own affairs in their own way be it in health, education, media, economics, land management and so on. There are increasing numbers of Indigenous graduates, academics, professionals and researchers who have the capability and knowledge to bring our voices and perspectives to the dominant mainstream fields and disciplines and push back the boundaries to be inclusive of Aboriginal knowledges, languages and culture. Working in research and tertiary education is not a chore, task, or job, rather it is a privilege and an honour to sit in positions of influence and look for and create opportunities to make a difference to the lives of Aboriginal and Torres Strait Islander peoples. It is not a hard job, but it is a heart job that I consider to be very important and critical to the future of young Indigenous peoples.

Dr. Robyn Ober is a Mamu/Djirribal woman from Far North Queensland and a Lead Researcher at Batchelor Institute, Northern Territory. Her association with Batchelor Institute spans three decades. Robyn has been at the front line of the development of both-ways pedagogy, working to combine Indigenous and non-Indigenous ways of knowing, being and learning in teaching practice and in research. She has gathered awards for her teaching in Indigenous and both-ways higher education and vocational education training. Dr. Ober is a respected researcher in Indigenous educational leadership and both-ways teaching and learning, with her work appearing in conferences, journals and national reports. In her doctoral work, she investigated identity and culture expressed in and through Aboriginal English. Dr. Ober's expertise has been called upon in numerous consultancies on education delivery, both-ways education, Indigenous research methodologies in the Northern Territory, national and international Indigenous educational contexts.

Open Access This chapter is licensed under the terms of the Creative Commons Attribution 4.0 International License (http://creativecommons.org/licenses/by/4.0/), which permits use, sharing, adaptation, distribution and reproduction in any medium or format, as long as you give appropriate credit to the original author(s) and the source, provide a link to the Creative Commons license and indicate if changes were made.

The images or other third party material in this chapter are included in the chapter's Creative Commons license, unless indicated otherwise in a credit line to the material. If material is not included in the chapter's Creative Commons license and your intended use is not permitted by statutory regulation or exceeds the permitted use, you will need to obtain permission directly from the copyright holder.

A Letter to All the Deadly Accidental Academics Starting Their Early Career Researcher Journey

Katrina Thorpe

1 Dear Deadly Accidental Academics and Now ECRs

Congratulations on completing your Ph.D.—it's wonderful to be in your ECR Company! As I write this letter to you, I'm in the final year of a Postdoctoral Research Fellowship at the Centre for the Advancement of Indigenous Knowledges (CAIK), University of Technology Sydney (UTS). If you're like me and have accidently stumbled into an academic career, I'm writing to you to say please 'own' that ECR title—it's your time to focus on your research trajectory.[1] My ECR journey has flown—so as it draws to a close, it's a timely opportunity to share some insights from my experience. I'll also reflect on the expectations I had on commencing my Postdoctoral Research Fellowship alongside the realities of my experience. Before I begin though, it's important to take a moment to position myself within Country.

I'm Associate Professor Katrina Thorpe, a Worimi woman who has lived on Gadigal Wangal Land (Inner West of Sydney) for close to three decades. I'd like to acknowledge the power and beauty of Gadigal–Wangal Land and pay my respects to Aboriginal and Torres Strait Islander Elders, community, and educators who have worked tirelessly to create the personal and professional opportunities that I now enjoy. I am indebted to my local Aboriginal community and to Gadigal–Wangal Country as it continues to nourish my life and family. It is Gadigal–Wangal Land that has inspired my teaching and research in the area of 'Learning from Country in the City', facilitating connections between students and Aboriginal people, communities, and Country in Sydney (Thorpe et al., 2021).

---

[1] If you happen to be a Deadly Accidental Academic who is yet to undertake a Ph.D., please don't wait too long, we need to build a critical mass of Aboriginal ECRs doing deadly Aboriginal-led research.

K. Thorpe (✉)
Nura Gili: Centre for Indigenous Programs, UNSW, Sydney, NSW, Australia
e-mail: k.thorpe@unsw.edu.au

© The Author(s) 2025
M. Trudgett et al. (eds.), *Indigenous Early Career Researchers in Australian Universities*, SpringerBriefs in Education,
https://doi.org/10.1007/978-981-97-2823-7_4

2 Long Story Short on Becoming an Accidental Academic—Early Experiences

I became an accidental academic over two decades ago when I started a second undergraduate degree in Aboriginal Studies at the University of Newcastle (UoN). My tutor, Ann Flood was a visiting Ngiyampaa academic from the University of Sydney. After learning that I had completed a Bachelor of Education, Ann suggested that I might be interested in applying for a position as a tutor at the Koori Centre, University of Sydney. It seemed like a great opportunity, so I applied and moved to Sydney. The Koori Centre was an autonomous Indigenous centre responsible for the academic support of Indigenous students and Indigenous Studies/Education. When I started, I taught 'mainstream' mandatory and elective Aboriginal education subjects but over time became involved in the Aboriginal education programs coordinated by the Koori Centre. These included the Diploma of Education (Aboriginal) and Bachelor of Education (Aboriginal Studies) Away-from-Base programs for Indigenous students, a suite of subjects in the Indigenous Studies Major for the (then) Faculty of Arts and mandatory Indigenous education/health units embedded in the university's education and nursing degrees.

When I reflect on this time and now having come face-to-face with the *benefit of hindsight*, it seems obvious that the development of an Indigenous research culture was in its infancy. We were a team of accidental academics who were inducted into the university's teaching and learning systems but not encouraged to participate in the parallel and somewhat mysterious world of academic research. 'Research' was something that happened 'out there'—somewhere else. Teaching non-Indigenous students about Indigenous Australia and ensuring that Aboriginal students were supported both academically and culturally at university was the focus of our work. Needless to say, I have no regrets in regard to these endeavours however, mentoring and a supportive research culture for academic staff would have had a profound impact on my research trajectory during the early stages of my career. It's interesting to read Cleverley and Mooney's (2010) history of the Koori Centre which discusses how a deficit budget led to the dissolution of the Koori Centre's research committee just before I commenced my Associate Lecturer position. They state that, 'Its [the Koori Centre's] research activity was singled out for pre-emptive savings, because its work was not considered essential for teaching or support and its appointees were short term' (p. 189). While this event occurred just a few years before I was employed, it seems the seeds were sown for prioritising teaching over research. At that time, Koori Centre staff argued that the university's Research Committee (handed the responsible for leading Indigenous research) underestimated the sustained effort required to build research capacity arguing that, 'The effort to achieve the outcomes has not been easy or straightforward. It has required skill and determination, and a vision based on realistic and achievable goals' (pp. 189–190). Clevereley and Mooney lament that 'The axe fell irrespective' (p. 190), research staff were let go, and Koori Centre research was reduced or terminated which 'broke up a team five years in the making' (p. 190).

3 My Experiences of Becoming an Indigenous ECR and Postdoctoral Research Fellow

Oddly, I didn't know what an ECR was until some months after I completed my Ph.D. I was introduced to the concept of an ECR through learning about postdoctoral research opportunities. It needs to be said that I had not intended to depart the institution that I had dedicated much of my career to. As a Lecturer, I worked with a fantastic team of Aboriginal and non-Aboriginal colleagues (all ECRs at the time of my graduation) and I enjoyed the teaching. However, the opportunity to undertake a Postdoctoral Research Fellowship in an Indigenous centre that valued and supported Indigenous-led research was profoundly important and enticing at this stage of my career.

Indeed, universities are wise to consider targeting Indigenous Postdoctoral Fellowships so that deadly accidental academics can map out their research pathway. In the institution where I once worked and studied, there wasn't a clear path to *'grow your own'* Postdoctoral Indigenous Research Fellows for employed staff. If *you* want to remain at your institution where you are currently employed and undertaking a Ph.D., it's worth asking questions about postdoctoral pathways for Indigenous ECRs. If there isn't suitable Postdoctoral Research Fellowship where you are currently working—there will be at other institutions—approach those institutions.

4 Great Expectations

Prior to completing my doctorate, teaching Indigenous Studies to mostly non-Indigenous student cohorts had been the focus of my time and energy. The shift to a research focused position meant that I had a very clear expectation that my Postdoctoral Research Fellowship would enable me to grow my capabilities as a researcher and contribute to Indigenous-led education research agendas. A personal goal was to conduct research that centred Aboriginal voices in the area I am most passionate—'Learning from Country' in preservice teacher education. In joining CAIK, I expected to join a collegial workplace surrounded by supportive Indigenous and non-Indigenous colleagues and mentors. I envisaged this work environment would be an authentic 'community-of-practice' (Wenger, 2000) and in this community-of-practice, our shared activities would be enabling for each person as while our research interests differ, we all share a commitment to Indigenist research (Rigney, 1999) and enacting Indigenous research methodologies. As a member of this community-of-practice, I hoped to spend more time working with local Aboriginal communities, developing relationships, sharing resources and our passions (Wenger, 2000) to create educational, social, and cultural impact in learning from and on Country. Beyond these goals, I was also looking forward to being part of a team that supervised and mentored the next generation of Indigenous HDRs.

5 Realities

Like life itself, some of the expectations I had as an ECR were realised, and others were not. When you're an ECR, there are many roles to juggle at any one time and sometimes this can be overwhelming. These roles will expand beyond the research goals you had in mind (such as research co-design, field research, writing grants and dissemination of research) and likely include a range activities and responsibilities such as teaching preparation, teaching classes, responding to student enquiries, dealing with resistant and sometimes racist students, marking, curriculum development, peer review of articles, supervision of HDR students, attending conferences, general administration and assisting colleagues to Indigenise the curriculum (to name a few). So how do you juggle all of these demands—particularly the juggle between teaching and research responsibilities? This is an increasing problem for many early career academics (see for example Bosanquet et al., 2017) and when coupled with the stress of dealing with resistant and racist students this can create emotional labour for Aboriginal academics (Asmar & Page, 2009). So while it's not easy to resolve the tensions around juggling teaching and research, I'll share some reflections on my experiences that were met while an ECR as well as the 'distractions' that were ever present.

6 Fulfilled Expectations

My expectations to carry out Indigenous-led research and be part of an authentic community-of-practice were realised. Since its inception, CAIK has been led by Aboriginal Professors who have successful research track records and it's a welcoming place for academics, doctoral, postdoctoral, and undergraduate students to meet in an informal collegial setting (whether in person or on 'Zoom' during the Covid-19 pandemic). When Covid-19 lockdowns impacted on my ability to undertake research yarns (Bessarab & Ng'andu, 2010) with preservice teachers and local Aboriginal communities, I was supported in developing a new project that has now opened unexpected and exciting teaching and research opportunities with local Aboriginal community members. During my fellowship I also had opportunities to collaborate with colleagues at other universities. One of these collaborations involved securing Category 3 funding (Category 3 income in this instance refers to contract income from Australian industry) with a large Australian non- government organisation that works closely with Aboriginal peoples and communities. Furthermore, working with colleagues from other universities enabled me to contribute to four Australian Research Council (ARC) grant applications. Three of these applications were unsuccessful but the fourth, an ARC linkage grant was successful. ARC grants are competitive and notoriously difficult to win so don't be disillusioned if unsuccessful the first few times you apply. Also consider the possibility of re-shaping these applications for other grants opportunities. Suffice to say, I'm excited about the opportunities and impact the ARC linkage grant will provide for all involved. I'm appreciative of the support I've received from Aboriginal and non-Aboriginal academics at UTS and other Australian universities who have grown my research experience. These people have become important mentors.

7 Some Possible 'Distractions' from Your Research

The work of embedding Indigenous graduate attributes within university curricular (sometimes referred to as 'Indigenising the curriculum') is an enormous task and as an Indigenous ECR you will likely be drawn into some of these processes. You may experience these requests as opportunities for growth and leadership, yet at other times these requests will be *extractive and even exhausting* engagements that may assist colleagues and the institution yet be invisible and undervalued work not recognised when your time as an ECR draws to a close. Try to be mindful of these requests and ensure that they don't distract you from your research plans.

Dr. Chelsea Watego, a Munanjahli and South Sea Islander woman reminds us of the exhaustion bound up in teaching whitefella's how 'to see our humanity' (Watego, 2021, p. 190) and for many Aboriginal academics this equates to dealing with racism in the classroom. If you haven't yet read Dr Watego's, book, *Another Day in the Colony,* please do. Watego highlights the multiple ways institutions maintain Aboriginal 'busy' work for the colony and in academia which hijack our research agendas and forcefully reminds us of the importance of holding ground and standing firm from the standpoint of Aboriginal people's self-determination and sovereignty. It so important to be strong in your boundaries and learn to say 'no' to the requests of your time that will distract you from the research that will have the most impact for you and the communities with which you work in service for (Watego, 2021, p. 140). If you can learn this skill during your time as an ECR, you will have a more productive research career.

8 A Brief Word on Research Systems

When you're employed at a university and undertaking research there's no escaping research bureaucracy and systems. While these systems might at times drive you to distraction, they are part of life as an academic researcher. When you start your research, it's important to keep in contact with your research office and engage in professional development opportunities to understand these processes and how they will assist you in administering your research grants. Naturally, research grants have conditions for expenditure of funds so it's important to understand these upfront. While not an exhaustive list, some starter questions that you could ask your research office include: Do you have budgeting tools (e.g., spreadsheets) to assist in keeping track of all the costs for my project? What are the "oncosts" that need to be included if I employ a research assistant? Can I role over the research funding from one year to the next? If not, what are the deadlines for acquitting funding? What happens with the money if I don't spend it? Knowing how to answer these questions is important in planning and working out contingencies if some aspects of your project require adaptation or are delayed due to extenuating circumstances. As my research was impacted by Covid-19 lockdowns, these questions were important in regard to understanding the processes for requesting approval to roll-over funds and subsequently ensuring that yearly expenditure deadlines were met.

9 Some Final Thoughts

Writing this letter to you has provided an opportunity to reflect on my journey from an accidental academic to an ECR. While moving to another university can provide opportunities for promotion, professional development, and widening professional teaching and research networks, a commitment to 'growing their own' Indigenous researchers should be a priority for research leaders in Australian universities. This means that pathways need to be developed and clearly articulated to Indigenous students from undergraduate study through to postdoctoral research opportunities. So my departing observation, Deadly Academic, is that if the university where you are currently working is not adequately supporting the growth of Indigenous ECRs, it's important to provide this feedback to change the workplace research culture. Also seek out mentors and Indigenous researcher networks (possibly outside of your institution) who will support and encourage your ECR journey. Being an ECR is a brief but important time in your academic career. Stay strong—I wish you well.

Associate Professor Katrina Thorpe

References

Asmar, C., & Page, S. (2009). Sources of satisfaction and stress among indigenous academic teachers: Findings from a national Australian study. *Asia Pacific Journal of Education, 29*(3), 387–401. https://doi.org/10.1080/02188790903097505

Bessarab, D., & Ng'andu, B. (2010). Yarning about yarning as a legitimate method in indigenous research. *International Journal of Critical Indigenous Studies, 3*(1), 37–50.

Bosanquet, A., Mailey, A., Matthews, K. E., & Lodge, J. M. (2017). Redefining 'early career' in academia: A collective narrative approach. *Higher Education Research & Development, 36*(5), 890–902.

Cleverley, J., & Mooney, J. (2010). *Taking our place: Aboriginal education and the story of the Koori Centre at the University of Sydney*. Sydney University Press.

Rigney, L.-I. (1999). Internationalization of an indigenous anticolonial cultural critique of research methodologies: A guide to Indigenist research methodology and its principles. *WICAZO SA Review, 14*(2), 109–121.

Thorpe, K., Burgess, C., & Egan, S. (2021). Aboriginal community-led preservice teacher education: Learning from country in the City. *Australian Journal of Teacher Education, 46*(1), 55–73.

Watego, C. (2021). *Another day in the colony*. University of Queensland Press.

Wenger, E. (2000). Communities of practice and social learning systems. *Organization, 7*(2), 225–246. https://doi.org/10.1177/135050840072002

Associate Professor Katrina Thorpe (Worimi) is the inaugural Chancellor's Postdoctoral Indigenous Research Fellow at the Centre for the Advancement of Indigenous Knowledges, University of Technology Sydney. Katrina has 25 years' experience teaching mandatory Indigenous Studies within the fields of education, social work, nursing, health and community development. Drawing on these diverse teaching experiences, Katrina's research has engaged the voices of Aboriginal community members, pre-service teachers and teacher educators to provide deeper understandings of the experiences that support or inhibit student learning and development of a personal and professional commitment to Indigenous education.

Open Access This chapter is licensed under the terms of the Creative Commons Attribution 4.0 International License (http://creativecommons.org/licenses/by/4.0/), which permits use, sharing, adaptation, distribution and reproduction in any medium or format, as long as you give appropriate credit to the original author(s) and the source, provide a link to the Creative Commons license and indicate if changes were made.

The images or other third party material in this chapter are included in the chapter's Creative Commons license, unless indicated otherwise in a credit line to the material. If material is not included in the chapter's Creative Commons license and your intended use is not permitted by statutory regulation or exceeds the permitted use, you will need to obtain permission directly from the copyright holder.

Navigation

Am I There Yet? Learning as I Go and Wondering What Success Looks Like

Michelle Locke

Warami (Hello),

I begin this chapter by introducing myself to you. I am known as Michelle, Dr. Locke, Dr. Mum, daughter, sister, aunt, niece, friend, colleague, I think you get the picture. My connection to Country is through my maternal Grandmother, Winifred Olive Locke, which can be traced back to Goomberi. He was Kuradji, (chief) of the Boorooberongal clan of the Dharug Nation. Bolongaia, (or Maria Lock as she is named in colonial records) is Goomberi's granddaughter and my four times great-grandmother (Locke, 2018). I am the eldest of four children, and a Mum to two deadly boys. I grew up in public housing not knowing about my connection to Dharug Country but with beliefs, values and spirit taught and practiced by Mum and her Mum, grounded in Dharug ways of knowing, being and doing, but those are personal stories for another time. As the eldest of four I did my best to follow the rules, avoid trouble and look after my siblings, who often complained that I was too bossy, which is probably mostly true. I liked the social connections that school offered, and I stuck with my studies because from a young age I decided that I really wanted to be a preschool teacher. Teaching is my thing, I am pretty sure that's why I am here, although now at the age of fifty-three I view the role of teaching very differently to the image in my head as girl of fifteen.

Despite earning a Diploma in Teaching (Early Childhood), a Bachelor of Education (Early Childhood) in 1992 and 1995 respectively at University of Western Sydney (although it had a different name back then) and a Master's Degree in Indigenous Education in 2016 from Macquarie University, I have to admit to not being well versed in the machinations of tenured employment in the academy. When I began as an Indigenous Higher Degree Research (HDR) student in February 2017, (at 47 years of age), I was most fortunate to be enrolled in the Centre for the Advancement of

---

M. Locke (✉)
Western Sydney University, Kingswood, NSW, Australia
e-mail: m.locke@westernsydney.edu.au

© The Author(s) 2025
M. Trudgett et al. (eds.), *Indigenous Early Career Researchers in Australian Universities*, SpringerBriefs in Education,
https://doi.org/10.1007/978-981-97-2823-7_5

Indigenous Knowledges (CAIK) at the University of Technology Sydney (UTS). In CAIK I had regular access to experienced Indigenous academics who were generous with their time and knowledge. It was a highly collegial space, and I thoroughly enjoyed the many opportunities to interact, work and collaborate with a variety of Indigenous HDR students and Indigenous staff. CAIK literally provided a physically and intellectually safe space where I could grow and learn as I progressed through my Ph.D. candidature. However, it was not until about halfway through my Ph.D. that I learned securing a permanent position at a university was not guaranteed on completion. This may sound naïve but like many other Indigenous students I am first in family to attend university (Barney, 2013; Fredericks & White, 2018; Locke et al., 2021), which meant that there wasn't anyone in my family who could provide experienced insights or advice. Having said this, it's important to say that although they had not attended a university themselves, the unrelenting support and encouragement I received from my mum, sister, Dharug family, and my own children was paramount to my success in earning a Ph.D. qualification.

1 Study, Teaching and Research

In January 2020, twelve months before the conferral of my Ph.D. I was fortunate to secure a six-month contract (that was later extended to the end of that year), as a Research Officer on a three-year longitudinal study at Western Sydney University (WSU). I felt nervous but optimistic about the move from UTS back to WSU. I was excited and felt rather accomplished as I was assigned my own office in the Badanami Centre for Indigenous Education. I thoroughly enjoyed meeting and yarning with Badanami staff and students, who were all so welcoming and made me feel at home from my first day. As the only academic staff member in the centre, I was also eager to begin meeting and collaborating with Indigenous academics across WSU's campuses. Unfortunately, this was halted by the Covid-19 pandemic that saw campuses across Australia close, and university staff and students forced to work and study from home. Although, Senior Indigenous staff and WSU executive provided much support to all staff and students, through a variety of means, I could probably still write a paper on the negative impacts of Covid-19. The main focus of that paper would undoubtably be on what my sister and I have labelled, 'impending doom syndrome', which quietly infiltrates self-confidence and plants seeds of imminent pain and failure even in the strongest and most positive of minds. But that too is a different story maybe for another day.

Though it's worth noting that the onset of Covid-19 in Australia also coincided with the beginning of my role as Research Officer on the *Developing Indigenous Early Career Researchers* project. So, my ambition and enthusiasm to travel Australia meeting, yarning and interviewing Indigenous Early Career Researchers (ECRs) was swiftly curtailed. Fortunately, 'zoom' enabled the research project and my ability to pay my rent and feed my family to continue.

Covid-19 aside and early into the project's second year, my Ph.D. was conferred. At that time, I applied and was fortunately successful in continuing my employment on the same research project but with a promotion to Postdoctoral Research Fellow. While this may appear as all smooth sailing it's fair to say that there were a number of personal and professional challenges (not including the pandemic) on the way to that stage in my academic career. Although my efforts, experiences and responsibilities as a Research Officer over the first 12 months of the project put me in good stead for the promotion, there was one particular aspect, I needed to significantly build upon as a new Early Career Researcher.

2 Publish, Publish, Publish

I was once told by a very supportive and generous non-Indigenous scholar who at the time employed me as a Research Assistant that: 'the currency of the academy is publication. If you wish to succeed in the academy'. He advised, 'you must publish, publish, publish'. At the time, I was studying a Masters in Indigenous Education and although I thought I understood the message, the gravity and complexity of this reality was completely lost on me. I can honestly say that the last three years have been a very steep learning curve, that involved a whole new vocabulary associated with employment positions, research grants and expectations of an academic research career. Acronyms for differing positions, departments and policies, measures for teaching workloads and research outputs, were just a few of the concepts I had not come into contact with previously or else did not fully understand.

At this point it is probably worth sharing that at the conferral of my Ph.D. my academic strengths were significantly grounded in teaching, with many years in various roles in early childhood settings, Transition to Schools Programs,[1] to lecturing and tutoring education units at TAFE[2] and universities. Thus, I was advised by a number of Indigenous academics that to secure a permanent position in a university I needed to focus my energy on building a sound publication record. I must confess to the fact that even at the time of writing this piece I find the definition and attainment of a sound publication record to be somewhat elusive. As an Indigenous HDR student I believed that the number and variety of publications, such as journal articles, chapters in books or even an entire book would provide proof of a sound if not proficient publication record. However, as an Indigenous ECR I have come to understand that this is a rather simplified view of what it is to be published as an

---

[1] The Transitions to School Program is offered once per week, at a local school in NSW, for children who were to be enrolled in kindergarten the following school year.

[2] TAFE stands for Technical and Further Education. It is a tertiary training institution mostly for trades and apprenticeships.

academic and of the stresses, challenges, wins and losses that arise when navigating this treacherous leviathan.

I have come to see that universities can be very competitive spaces that often value Western based knowledges and beliefs over others (Fredericks, 2011; Thunig & Jones, 2020). I have also learned that including Indigenous Knowledges in universities is often open to non-Indigenous questions and critiques that can undermine or silence Indigenous values and perspectives (Baice et al., 2021; Kidman & Chu, 2017; Walter & Butler, 2013). This means, that my efforts to build a sound publication record as an Indigenous ECR requires specialised skills and tenacity. I need to find a way to meet institutional requirements whilst at the same time respectfully raise the voices of Dharug peoples in my community and advocate the voices of Indigenous and First Nations peoples more broadly.

Much literature cites a definitive relationship between a successful academic career and research outputs in the form of publications (Asmar & Page, 2018; Fredericks, 2011; Staniland et al., 2019). Aprile et al. (2021) states that in Australia, 'the publish or perish adage is alive and well' (p. 1131) and this rings true to the advice I have received regarding my publication record. However, I have found navigating publication expectations and processes to be challenging, disheartening and sometimes rewarding. The need and pressure to publish is a reality of academic recognition and success for all scholars, however there are without doubt additional barriers and challenges Indigenous academics must negotiate, navigate and on occasion concede. This point was clearly identified and explained by Indigenous and First Nation scholars Fredericks (2011) and Staniland et al. (2019) who note the challenge of publishing in journals that are highly ranked but expect Indigenous voices to be palatable to a mostly non-Indigenous readership. On the other hand, Indigenous scholars can choose to publish in Indigenous journals that raise Indigenous issues from Indigenous perspectives but are ranked much lower so offer less chance of academic security or promotion.

For myself the most important factor when writing a paper from the findings of an Indigenous research project such as *Developing Indigenous Early Career Researchers* is to ensure I am genuinely honouring and representing the voices of all those Indigenous participants who were brave and generous enough to share their truths, experiences, and wealth of knowledge. This involves an ongoing conversation with myself (sometimes even out loud), that guides me through a process of checking and double checking that what I have written will effectively and respectively raise Indigenous voices and champion the value and validity of Indigenous Knowledges, skills and strengths in an arena where they are often misinterpreted, underestimated or silenced.

As an Indigenous ECR I am accountable to truth telling and to honouring and celebrating the voices of Indigenous and First Nations peoples on whose shoulders I stand. I am also determined to support and build pathways for the voices, Knowledges and aspirations of my Indigenous colleagues and peers. With this in mind I encourage all scholars to read, share and cite the works of Indigenous ECRs and scholars. We have much to share that is of benefit to everyone living, working, studying or visiting our Countries.

Finally, in thinking about my approach to navigating publication from within the academy I decided that a poem would be the best way to offer some insight into my thoughts and feelings in my endeavour to write something of value. Although I labelled it as a process it is important to understand that my thinking is not linear and that my approach often involves visiting and revisiting many questions. Usually, my indicator of knowing when to pass a paper onto another person for review is after I have visited each question multiple times and have exhausted all answers available to me. Perhaps sharing a bit of my journey so far will help alleviate some of the stress that other Indigenous ECRs might experience in the academy.

Didjurigura yana jannawi bubuwul ingami

Thank you for walking with me and strengthening my spirit.

Always Turning, Sometimes Spinning

WHAT
do Indigenous Early Career Researchers bring to the academy,
do non-Indigenous scholars recognise or understand,
do universities underestimate or overlook,
is hidden or silenced,
is valued?

WHICH
journals to target,
theories to engage,
style to write,
Knowledges to engage,
people to speak back to,
stories to protect,
stories to tell?

WHO
is speaking, reading,
watching, sharing, learning,
taking, judging,
understanding, changing,
strengthened, questioned,
is listening?

HOW BEST TO
honour and champion Indigenous voices,
break barriers,
build reciprocal networks,
challenge assumptions,
stay strong, be brave, celebrate, recognise,
stand out, stand up, advocate,
effect change?

WHEN WILL THIS PUBLICATION BE
articulate, sound, worthy, interesting,
creative, engaging, thought provoking,
life changing, published, counted,
ENOUGH?
BREATH, LISTEN, REPEAT

References

Aprile, K. T., Ellem, P., & Lole, L. (2021). Publish, perish, or pursue? Early career academics' perspectives on demands for research productivity in regional universities. *Higher Education Research & Development, 40*(6), 1131–1145. https://doi.org/10.1080/07294360.2020.1804334

Asmar, C., & Page, S. (2018). Pigeonholed, peripheral or pioneering? Findings from a national study of Indigenous Australian academics in the disciplines. *Studies in Higher Education, 43*(9), 1679–1691. https://doi.org/10.1080/03075079.2017.1281240

Baice, T., Lealaiauloto, B., Meiklejohn-Whiu, S., Fonua, S. M., Allen, J. M., Matapo, J., Iosefo, F., & Fa'avae, D. (2021). Responding to the call: Talanoa, va-vā, early career network and enabling academic pathways at a university in New Zealand. *Higher Education Research & Development, 40*(1), 75–89. https://doi.org/10.1080/07294360.2020.1852187

Barney, K. (2013). 'Taking your mob with you': Giving voice to the experiences of Indigenous Australian postgraduate students. *Higher Education Research & Development, 32*(4), 515–528. https://doi.org/10.1080/07294360.2012.696186

Fredericks, B. (2011). Universities are not the safe place we would like to think they are, but they are getting safer': Indigenous women academics in higher education. *Journal of Australian Indigenous Issues, 14*(1), 41–53.

Fredericks, B., & White, N. (2018). Using bridges made by others as scaffolding and establishing footings for those that follow: Indigenous women in the Academy. *Australian Journal of Education, 62*(3), 243–255. https://doi.org/10.1177/0004944118810017

Kidman, J., & Chu, C. (2017). Scholar outsiders in the neoliberal university: Transgressive academic labour in the Whitestream. *New Zealand Journal of Educational Studies, 52*(1), 7–19. https://doi.org/10.1007/s40841-017-0079-y

Locke, M. L. (2018). Wirrawi Bubuwul—Aboriginal women strong. *The Australian Journal of Education, 62*(3), 299–310. https://doi.org/10.1177/0004944118799483

Locke, M. L., Trudgett, M., & Page, S. (2021). Indigenous Early Career Researchers—Creating pearls in the academy. *Australian Educational Researcher*. https://doi.org/10.1007/s13384-021-00485-1

Staniland, N. A., Harris, C., & Pringle, J. K. (2019). Fit for whom? Career strategies of Indigenous (Maori) academics. *Higher Education, 79*(4), 589–604. https://doi.org/10.1007/s10734-019-00425-0

Thunig, A., & Jones, T. (2020). 'Don't make me play house-n***er': Indigenous academic women treated as 'black performer' within higher education. *Australian Educational Researcher*, 397–417. https://doi.org/10.1007/s13384-020-00405-9

Walter, M., & Butler, K. (2013). Teaching race to teach Indigeneity. *Journal of Sociology, 49*(4), 397–410. https://doi.org/10.1177/1440783313504051

Dr. Michelle Locke is a Boorooberongal woman of the Dharug Nation, a very proud Mum of two boys and Western Sydney University alumnus. From Jan 2020 to Dec 2022 Michelle was employed firstly as a Professional Researcher and following conferral of her Ph.D. in 2021 as a Postdoctoral Research Fellow with the Office of Deputy Vice-Chancellor Indigenous Leadership on the *Developing Indigenous Early Career Researchers* ARC project. In January 2023 Michelle commenced in the position of Senior Lecturer in the School of Education at Western Sydney University.

Open Access This chapter is licensed under the terms of the Creative Commons Attribution 4.0 International License (http://creativecommons.org/licenses/by/4.0/), which permits use, sharing, adaptation, distribution and reproduction in any medium or format, as long as you give appropriate credit to the original author(s) and the source, provide a link to the Creative Commons license and indicate if changes were made.

The images or other third party material in this chapter are included in the chapter's Creative Commons license, unless indicated otherwise in a credit line to the material. If material is not included in the chapter's Creative Commons license and your intended use is not permitted by statutory regulation or exceeds the permitted use, you will need to obtain permission directly from the copyright holder.

Musings About Work-Life Balance

Tracy Woodroffe

1 Who I Am

My name is Dr Tracy Woodroffe. I am a mum, a wife, a daughter, a sister, and an aunt. I am an educator, a researcher, and a colleague. My cultural heritage is Aboriginal, White Australian, Irish, Scottish, and Swedish. I was raised and identify as Aboriginal but I believe that the labels given to us by others don't define who we are. They make it easier for others to put us in neat little boxes and often keep us in those boxes for their convenience. Labelling can only result in limitations. I object to constraints placed on me by others. I define my life and the possibilities in that.

2 How I Feel

If COVID has taught us anything, it has taught us the importance of perspective and making time for the essential thing in our lives—our family. This isn't necessarily the focus I had at the beginning of my HDR journey. At that time, I felt strongly that I had to spend as much time on my research as possible because there was a need to get the work done quickly, and the matter under investigation was urgent. Now with the benefit of hindsight, I understand things differently. The journey that I am on is not linear. It involves reflection and evolves through a series of developments, circling back around to discover something else. Things happen simultaneously, with activities overlapping and not neatly occurring one after the other. Sometimes I am ready to learn the lessons at hand, and sometimes it takes a while.

I feel that these developments can be seen in the progression of my publications, research, lecturing, supervision and community engagement but I am not sure if it is

---

T. Woodroffe (✉)
Charles Darwin University, Casuarina, NT, Australia
e-mail: tracy.woodroffe@cdu.edu.au

© The Author(s) 2025
M. Trudgett et al. (eds.), *Indigenous Early Career Researchers in Australian Universities*, SpringerBriefs in Education,
https://doi.org/10.1007/978-981-97-2823-7_6

something that anyone else notices. The progression has developed into an academic track record, which is apparently quite successful for an Early Career Researcher. Before I had the beginnings of a track record, I had over twenty years of industry experience to justify and establish my authority in my chosen field. My lecturing responsibilities further underscored my educational knowledge and expertise and confirmed my authority to speak about Indigenous engagement. My PhD topic was a personal quest to expose the knowledge gap that would liberate Indigenous students and educators and change the Westernised Australian education system to be more inclusive. My publications and further research projects have continued to focus on this goal. My purpose is obvious to me but not necessarily realised by others.

3 How I Do What I Do

My work has steadily unfolded from my PhD research beginnings and developed into central themes, expanding to further research. Standpoint and methodology, pedagogy and teacher education, Indigenous education and engagement, cultural reflexivity and workforce development are the unfolding areas of focus. They could be described as the links between the Australian education system and Indigenous peoples and Knowledges. As stated before like the progression in my career development, these themes have not developed in a linear way, often overlapping and circling back around. All the while, I have felt that most people don't necessarily see me or my potential or, don't notice because they are caught up in their own journeys. I understand this and I have come to realise that I must be my advocate with my best interests and, by extension, my family's best interests at heart. Therefore, at work, I am required to be vigilant. This constant vigilance added to the work required of a female Indigenous researcher and lecturer is exhausting, and because of that, I must separate work time from family time. Family and home are sanctuaries that must be treasured and nurtured. No matter how many times I change my workplace or profession, family is the centre that the rest of the universe rotates around.

So, it is true that work needs to fit with the family. As a mum and a wife, I work to live and not the other way around. My education, skills, and knowledge are an advantage to benefit my family. At the same time, I enjoy the intellectual challenge and the pay that I get to bring home, but with my skill set, if work doesn't fit with family, I will change position so that it does. Family comes first always. This acknowledgement and realisation have empowered me to be confident about making changes to my professional career as required. Each time I make a change is an opportunity to learn something new, work differently, and do that with different people. I learn from that experience. Nothing is wasted. Challenge is a learning opportunity. The resulting reflexive practice helps me work through future challenges and keep looking forward to what will come next. Consequently, I choose not to be limited or defined by other people's opinions or attitudes. I think about what is best for me in my career development and determine how my decisions benefit my family most. If appropriate professional development is not offered, I have found my own in areas that I deem appropriate for my profession and interests. An example of this is taking up martial arts and achieving a black belt to build confidence and strength. I am currently studying an online course to widen my career options. I have ambitions to dabble in different fields and broaden my opportunities.

4 What I Know

I am confident that I know 'me' best. The saying 'she knew she could and then she did' rings true to how I approach my life with the endeavour to be happy and strive to be a good person. I expect that this concept of what constitutes a 'good' person may mean something different for everyone. I think that there is still a common thread. What it means at the core is for all of us to try and be better than we already are. Better than what exactly? If we could define that, it would be too easy to achieve. Being a good person is like finding the gold at the rainbow's end. It looks possible but always is just out of reach and a lifelong goal. The point is that we wake up each day and have plans to achieve. Perspectives about those goals will be different, as will the judgement we place on ourselves about the degree to which those goals were achieved.

Don't mistake thinking that work pressures us to achieve goals. In part, it does, but in understanding the bigger picture, we all set standards for ourselves and work hard to live up to them. This can explain why we have too heavy a focus on professional life. We can spend too much time competing with peers and need to allow ourselves a balance and an outlet away from work. Our profession and work are not the whole of who we are. While this statement makes sense, the difficulty in academia is *reputation*. We build a professional reputation and *social capital* by building a track record. When we pivot or shift workplace or career, losing our professional identity can be debilitating. Starting fresh without the social capital built up over many years can make us feel insignificant or irrelevant. This can be countered by having a solid sense of self and believing in the sanctuary of family and home, trusting in the balance.

When I resigned from my previous job as a teacher to begin working as a university lecturer and researcher, I had what I thought was an identity crisis. It turned out to be not a cultural problem but a professional situation: I was reluctant to resign from the education department because I had always thought of myself as a teacher. I was advised by the HR officer that while on extended service leave, I was taking up a position that could be held by someone else and that the sooner I resigned, the better. This did not fit the department's rhetoric of increasing and supporting Indigenous educators. Unfortunately, the apparent lie of supporting and increasing Indigenous teacher numbers disillusioned me, which strengthened my resolve to lecture in teacher education and conduct research to investigate and expose educational disadvantages. It still came as a shock when my resignation was finalised. I wondered if I stopped being a teacher, I would lose a significant part of my identity as this was how I had identified for more than twenty years. This had been my identity for over twenty years. It took a little while, but I finally realised that I could be whatever I wanted to be, anywhere. My frame of mind and perspective were foundational to who I wanted to be and where I wanted that to happen. Being a teacher was not about a position and a position number. Being a teacher was about me and my skills, knowledge and experience. When I left, I didn't leave that behind. It came with me as an asset to my new role as a Lecturer and Researcher. I realised that I then had the impetus and ability to use my insider teacher knowledge to impact positive change in education for Indigenous students and teachers.

5 How I Choose to Live

So, here I am today as an accomplished educator who is much wiser than nine years ago. I have a successful compulsory school (Early Childhood, Primary and Secondary) teaching career spanning 23 years. The experience gained during that time has provided me with the credibility, reputation and knowledge to conduct research and publish in that field for the benefit of other Aboriginal people. I have been a Lecturer and Researcher for nine years, which means that I have been an educator for 32 years, over 60 per cent of my life. The truth is that I have been a learner for even longer. Each time I teach about something, I learn more about the content itself or from the students I teach. I accept that learning is a continuous process that keeps us motivated to engage and connect. Waning interest or motivation is a cue to learn about something new or to try to approach something differently. That is not to say that you will be great at everything you try or find out about, but the challenge is a motivating element of learning. For example, I have a passion for archaeology and was motivated to enroll in a course about History. In the course, the units covered were about The Tudors and the Stuarts, WWII Fascism and Nazis, and finally, Native American peoples in the US. Two out of the three topics sounded exciting to me, and I could connect or engage with them based on my current interests and knowledge. One of the topics sounded very dull and I found it to be more difficult to be engaged with. The mental stretch was not necessarily with the topics that interest me in this situation. The boring topic was the challenge that meant completing a tedious essay. If faced with a similar situation, it could be helpful to think about how you could broaden your knowledge and understanding to satisfy the assessment requirements and pass the course. Reflecting on the situation, could enable you to meet the challenge of learning about the perceived boring topic in a way that catches your interest. The strategy is to select the best essay question. Academia is very similar. For the most part, we have space to shape our work practices by choosing which areas to work in, who to invite onto a research team, and how to collaborate with colleagues in lecturing. The key is to be strategic and try to shape the environment you wish to work in. This may not be as easy as it sounds for everyone, but we can all be mindful when options arise and try to continue moving in the right direction.

6 In Conclusion

We all get through the daily grind to eventually spend time on the topics and activities that interest us. An alternative way of thinking about what we do as academics is to consider how to be more strategic in how you work each day. Ask yourself—what do you love to talk about? What are your areas of expertise? Are you happy with that? Would you like to know more about something else? What do you enjoy researching? How do you enjoy researching? Who do you enjoy working with, and why? And, when you are done with that, think about what it is that you want to do outside of work. How can you optimise your time with family? How is your health? What sport do you play? What are your other hobbies? Finally, ask yourself where your priority is. If it is heavily weighted towards work, you may be missing the point. Stopping to smell the roses may be just what you need to be healthier, happier, and less stressed to be engaged and productive at work. You know yourself best. Stop and reflect on your attitude towards a work-life balance, and if things need to change, do not be deterred by the challenge. Be enthused and engaged in making changes that will benefit you and your family.

Dr. Tracy Woodroffe is a Senior Lecturer and Coordinator in the Faculty of Arts and Society specialising in Education, Teaching Indigenous Learners and Indigenous Knowledge in Education. She is a local Warumungu Luritja woman with extensive experience in Early Childhood, Primary, Secondary and Tertiary classrooms. Dr. Woodroffe is interested in educational pedagogy, identity, perspective, and the use of Indigenous Knowledge in educational contexts. Her work includes Indigenous methodology through an Indigenous Women's Standpoint, and the use of Presentation Feedback.

Open Access This chapter is licensed under the terms of the Creative Commons Attribution 4.0 International License (http://creativecommons.org/licenses/by/4.0/), which permits use, sharing, adaptation, distribution and reproduction in any medium or format, as long as you give appropriate credit to the original author(s) and the source, provide a link to the Creative Commons license and indicate if changes were made.

The images or other third party material in this chapter are included in the chapter's Creative Commons license, unless indicated otherwise in a credit line to the material. If material is not included in the chapter's Creative Commons license and your intended use is not permitted by statutory regulation or exceeds the permitted use, you will need to obtain permission directly from the copyright holder.

The Everyday of Risk and Vulnerability: Being an Indigenous Early Career Researcher

Vincent Backhaus

In the many accounts of different participants identity journey's, there was evidence of the tensions described in Nakata's notion of the Cultural Interface as a complex space of converging discourses and contradictory, ambiguous and confused sets of meanings. (Carlson, 2016, p. 239).

1 People of Knowledge

Since completing my doctoral training in 2018, I have taught across the Indigenous Studies major at a regional university. In the second-year undergraduate subjects I helped develop during the same period since gaining the role, I have attempted to ensure students who undertake the subjects begin to engage in an understanding of Aboriginal and Torres Strait Islander peoples as a *People of Knowledge*. People of Knowledge as a broad second year theme teaches students how to consider Australia's First peoples through a history of knowing and producing knowledge. This knowledge comes from navigating a continuing everyday existence within the nation state and/or institutional environment that ruptures or reconstitutes continuities in sometimes discontinuous modalities (Nakata, 2007).

Students learn about how to develop their awareness through exposure to this rub and prepare their understanding of the ways Aboriginal and Torres Strait Islander peoples navigate this discontinuity within the present while acknowledging the continuity of the everyday. This demonstrates to students how historical assumptions about Aboriginal and Torres Strait Islander families, individuals, communities, and places

---

V. Backhaus (✉)
The Cairns Institute, Nguma Bada Campus, James Cook University, Smithfield, Cairns, QLD, Australia
e-mail: vincent.backhaus@jcu.edu.au

are challenged and resisted as part of a continuum of engagement rather than a static historicity. In delivering these subjects to my undergraduate students, what may feel to young-minded undergraduates like a conceptual puzzle, feels a little different and weighs a little heavier on my shoulders.

This heaviness is accounted for in the awareness I feel to honor and respect the Aboriginal and Torres Strait Islander and South Sea Story Lines embedded within my life while also accounting for the delivery of the same Story Lines in formal teaching and institutional environments. I am a Kalkadoon, Kiwai and Malaita man with familial connections across Queensland and the Pacific which means most if not all my family have and continue to experience the logics, narratives and impact of continuing institutional and State legacies in the everyday. This reflexive weight is observed in my understanding of the everyday of being an Early Career Researcher (ECR) also responding to the everyday of attending to academic administration, teaching, research, family and community commitments, Country and personal health. Being an ECR you have not necessarily curated a subjective difference or separation between yourself and your work—you become the subject matter just as the subject matter becomes you. Resultingly, you are at risk of being caught in an unsettling and reactive discursivity brought about by the institutional process of becoming an ECR through priorities and pressure points shaping your academic identity.

2 Ontologies of the Everyday—The Indigenous ECR Experience

Ontologies of the everyday contribute to the understanding that people never merely react or respond to what exists but agentively act in co-realising both the world and themselves (Stetsenko, 2019). In the context of this chapter, Aboriginal and Torres Strait Islander ECRs are positioned as pioneers rather than advocates: pioneers in that we tend to be the first into the spaces we inhabit in departments or colleges, creating rare opportunities for non-Indigenous colleagues to encounter our voice and response as compared to the words in scholarship or as research participants in research we may never have controlled or co-designed or co-led. We are situated at the forefront of developing, teaching, and guiding institutional mindsets whether we want to or not. We are exposed to this reality from the first days of our postdoctoral roles and contribute to a small, pre-existing, tired but dedicated and passionate critical mass of existing Aboriginal and Torres Strait Islander academics. We run the risk of doing things every day that are always new and making mistakes, repeating ourselves and not knowing why as well as opening us up to the vulnerabilities of being situated within a dynamic, continuous, unsettling and norm breaking environment.

I appreciate the tension and the long bow I draw in thinking of being human and being an Indigenous Australian and or an Indigenous ECR share a sameness. Some may argue that ECR experiences are universal and institutionally bound, and that *we* all face the same ECR challenges and hurdles whether you identify as Indigenous or non- Indigenous. I do find an incommensurability exists in such arguments especially when I account for the reflexive turn in being the subject that I teach. I could never be a static identity, partitioned and read about in books just as books and scholarship could never account for the identities that Aboriginal, Torres Strait and South Sea Islander peoples account for, and live through, and navigate in the everyday of being a People of Knowledge. This alludes to an alternative or special kind of personhood, and this is an important juncture. Developing an identifiable means or pathway with which to navigate a contested site of knowledge systems evident within Indigenous ECR environments or for that matter Aboriginal and Torres Strait Islander peoples is a necessary step in considering the kinds of personhoods Indigenous ECRs inhabit among many others. As Indigenous ECRs or Indigenous Australians we can never really be defined but are always becoming. This is in response to the reactive or proactive moments we navigate in the everyday of being a People of Knowledge with agential recourse to a remembered discontinuity in our realties.

I can acknowledge the challenge and difficulty of teaching and engaging with literature that pinpoints with accuracy this discontinuity through each epoch of Aboriginal and Torres Strait Islander engagement with the everyday through a depth of research and discourses. The discourse includes descriptions of frontier conflict, massacre, starvation, displacement, protectionism, stolen generation, marginalisation, health and gender implications, and the notion of the Aboriginal problem through a continuing assimilatory process (e.g. Attwood, 2017; Ellinghaus, 2003; Fredericks, 2008; Rose, 2011). These examples highlight the complexity and diversity of narratives that perhaps make us react to in various ways, and or discover alternative proactive pathways and strategies *through* these narratives to reflect upon rather than avoid or seek pathways around such stories of discontinuity.

I regularly arrive at a point towards the end of each semester feeling and knowing the literature and scholarship of my ECR craft impacts my family and the Story Line of my family and community. I see and feel a reconstituted self in the process as part of a continuing logic of who I am as person in the everyday of a socio-cultural milieu (Stetsenko, 2008) struggling to navigate the present and its intention towards Aboriginal and Torres Strait Islander peoples existence and futures. What I wish to argue is that traditional ECR roles are not distinct tangible co-realised positions for Aboriginal and Torres Strait Islander candidates and the academic institutions that recruit us. They are roles embodied within a thick subjectivity that impacts the ways you wish to create and realise forms of agency in the everyday and to see and realise impact. In other words, for me I am the institutional subject and the object taught. Whatever scholarship I attempt to place as a buffer between my sense of self and what I am described as, tends to be questioned and debated just as my existence is questioned and debated despite the goal of wanting to impart a shared understanding to the next generation and acknowledge and celebrate a doctoral qualification.

This understanding could be considered through the socio-cultural impact of how ECR identity threats are experienced (Callagher et al., 2021). Threats can be understood in the form of considering the potential harm to the value, meanings, or enactment of an academic identity (Petriglieri, 2011): in this context an identity and an expectation of an identity embodying a sense of Indigeneity. This includes but is not limited to being an Aboriginal, Torres Strait and/or South Sea Islander, being human, rationalising the logics of problematic and truthful scholarly discourse about Indigenous peoples, engaging with the privilege of being a credentialed Indigenous ECR, supporting family and community, and then capably determining some useful form of social emotional and physical well-being for my body in the list of priorities and expectations the body embraces. This can be quite disconcerting because as an ECR you necessarily do not operate with a known standard of evaluating what is important and what is a priority. This results in everything being important and everything being a priority. Summarily, an ontology of the everyday within the understanding of being an Indigenous ECR, is about learning the norms of academia, thinking about your priorities and pressure points while doing the significant work of developing a personhood during a dynamic period of an unsettled academic and professional identity making process.

I do want to get back to reading and writing, to do the things that drive me to write and as such rewrite, to contribute to, support and add to the likes of the *Unmapping project* (Birch, 2016) or *Untold stories* (Wright, 2019), *the Windrush songs* (Berry, 2007) and to expand and be bolder and raise questions about European thought on the South (Maldonado-Torres, 2004). These kinds of thoughts are invariably part of the development of a broader academic identity (Mula et al., 2021) at the beginning of potential future that navigates a tension of finding a community but also trying to define the community itself and finding yourself within a community (Lave & Wenger, 1991; Sweitzer, 2009)—within the everyday of being an ECR. This is accomplished by taking those risks, being vulnerable and being open to where new experiences might support or detract from that development and being okay with whatever is achieved and or expected at the time.

3 Power and Privilege of Being Indigenous ECRs

I think also about spending time to reflect on the privilege of being an Aboriginal and Torres Strait Islander ECR. Indeed, there is risk and vulnerability as well as erosion and reconstruction of professional and personal identities in this ECR *business*. However, the notion of privilege in this paper accounts for the need to be mindful of what this ECR role and responsibility means despite the challenges I have described, and the privilege embodied within such descriptions. The challenges to the development of an academic identity resonant with me (e.g. Mula et al., 2021; Signoret et al., 2019); yet the privilege of being able to say I have an academic identity let alone an ECR identity in need of development equally needs to be evaluated. Indigenous education itself is fraught with deficit approaches to teaching and learning and Aboriginal and Torres Strait Islander ECRs today are part of that conversation and part of the challenging production of knowledge to map out and continue the work of defining Indigenous futures. It raises questions around what kinds of engagements, futures, and conceptualisations you are responsible for and how you approach this kind of work.

This is significant because as contemporary trends suggest, we still as a postdoctoral cohort both internationally and domestically have a small number of doctoral completions and graduations in the country (Trudgett et al., 2016). Those of us who do progress through undergraduate, postgraduate, and doctoral achievement arrive at a rare and exclusive position. This informs our positionality and our standpoint and the development of what we would hope to achieve. What this means is to be mindful of our position as institutional and societal thought leaders and thinkers and our contribution to our standpoint as a People of Knowledge.

The implication of privilege is to be mindful of the kinds of pathways towards academic credentialing that is built on foundational legacies of others, inclusive of our families of whom at various times prior to our arrival as ECRs would not have even been considered for any credential let alone higher education opportunities. *First in family* to achieve is still a mantra echoed in our families, places, and communities. This is an implication of existing settler colonial narratives that highlights a diversity of places, demographics, and economic privileges a People of Knowledge have come to know and navigate. Remember we still have family living in former missions across the country, we still have family housed in a vast range of institutional places, we still have families who are disconnected from place. We also feel the impact of institutional mechanisms that process us and our families to anchor affective evaluations of individual and familial futures and what possibilities such futures may hold. These affective evaluations have real impacts on the ways we access and resource the agential capacity of our family and community legacies. Being mindful of this helps to empower what we do and how we approach our privilege from positions of knowledge and integrity.

4 Conclusion

In closing this small chapter contribution, the power and privilege of being called an Aboriginal and Torres Strait Islander ECR can feel heavy, and I would argue ought to feel that way. We need to be writing about and developing principles and guides for the next generation of ECRs. The evidence of a higher Indigenous Higher Degree Research (HDR) commencement rate as compared to HDR completion rates highlights Aboriginal and Torres Strait Islander ECRs continue to be a small critical mass within academic institutions. Gender disparity and the strengths and weaknesses of what regional or metropolitan institutional environments offer, add to the ways Aboriginal and Torres Strait Islander ECRs contribute to an ontology of the everyday through participating in the continuing construction(s) of a Peoples of Knowledge.

Acknowledgements Vincent Backhaus would like to acknowledge the support of the Charlie Perkins Scholarship.

References

Attwood, B. (2017). Denial in a settler society: The Australian case. *History Workshop Journal, 84*, 24–43. https://doi.org/10.1093/hwj/dbx029

Berry, J. (2007). *Windrush songs.* Bloodaxe Books.

Birch, T. (2016). The great unmapping project of 2016. *Griffith Review, 52*, 52–54.

Callagher, L. J., El Sahn, Z., Hibbert, P., Korber, S., & Siedlok, F. (2021). Early career researchers' identity threats in the field: The shelter and shadow of collective support. *Management Learning, 52*(4), 442–465. https://doi.org/10.1177/1350507621997738

Carlson, B. (2016). *The politics of identity: Who counts as Aboriginal today?* Aboriginal Studies Press.

Ellinghaus, K. (2003). Absorbing the "Aboriginal Problem": Controlling interracial marriage in Australia in the late 19th and early 20th centuries. *Aboriginal History, 27*, 183–207. https://doi.org/10.3316/ielapa.822408545360812

Fredericks, B. (2008). Researching with Aboriginal women as an Aboriginal woman researcher. *Australian Feminist Studies, 23*(55), 113–129. https://doi.org/10.1080/08164640701816272

Lave, J., & Wenger, E. (1991). Situated learning: Legitimate peripheral participation. *Cambridge University Press.* https://doi.org/10.1017/CBO9780511815355

Maldonado-Torres, N. (2004). The topology of being and the geopolitics of knowledge. *City, 8*(1), 29–56. https://doi.org/10.1080/1360481042000199787

Mula, J., Rodríguez, C. L., Domingo Segovia, J., & Cruz-González, C. (2021). Early career researchers' identity: A qualitative review. *Higher Education Quarterly.* https://doi.org/10.1111/hequ.12348

Nakata, M. (2007). The cultural interface. *Australian Journal of Indigenous Education, 36*(5), 2–14.

Petriglieri, J. L. (2011). Under threat: Responses to and the consequences of threats to individuals' identities. *The Academy of Management Review, 36*(4), 641–662.

Rose, D. (2011). Aboriginal life and death in Australian settler nationhood. *Aboriginal History Journal, 25.* https://doi.org/10.22459/AH.25.2011.09

Signoret, C., Ng, E., Da Silva, S., Tack, A., Voss, U., Lidö, H. H., Patthey, C., Ericsson, M., Hadrévi, J., & Balachandran, C. (2019). Well-being of early-career researchers: Insights from a Swedish survey. *Higher Education Policy, 32*(2), 273–296. https://doi-org.elibrary.jcu.edu.au/https://doi.org/10.1057/s41307-018-0080-1

Stetsenko, A. (2008). From relational ontology to transformative activist stance on development and learning: Expanding Vygotsky's (CHAT) project. *Cultural Studies of Science Education, 3*(2), 471–491. https://doi.org/10.1007/s11422-008-9111-3

Stetsenko, A. (2019). Radical-transformative agency: Continuities and contrasts with relational agency and implications for education. *Frontiers in Education, 4.* https://www.frontiersin.org/article/https://doi.org/10.3389/feduc.2019.00148

Sweitzer, V. (Baker). (2009). Towards a theory of doctoral student professional identity development: A developmental networks approach. *The Journal of Higher Education, 80*(1), 1–33. https://doi.org/10.1080/00221546.2009.11772128

Trudgett, M., Page, S., & Harrison, N. (2016). Brilliant minds: A snapshot of successful Indigenous Australian doctoral students. *The Australian Journal of Indigenous Education, 45*(1), 70–79. https://doi.org/10.1017/jie.2016.8

Wright, A. (2019). Literature: Telling the untold stories. *Overland, 234*, 16.

Dr. Vincent Backhaus completed his doctoral degree at The University of Cambridge, He matriculated from Trinity College, Cambridge in 2013. His graduate studies explored the connections between Traditional Knowledge and learning theory with a core focus on cognition and ways of teaching. He began post-doctoral work lecturing across the Indigenous Education and Research Centre (IERC) James Cook University, Indigenous studies undergraduate major and continues to supervise students undertaking the JCU MPhil, and the Ph.D. Indigenous HDR program. Vincent is currently a Research Fellow in the Cairns Institute with co-investigators Associate Prof Felecia Watkin Lui and Professor Stewart Lockie working with Traditional Owners across the Great Barrier Reef to consider meaningful engagement with Great Barrier Reef Marine Park Authority and on water industry in the governance, care and management of Sea Country.

Open Access This chapter is licensed under the terms of the Creative Commons Attribution 4.0 International License (http://creativecommons.org/licenses/by/4.0/), which permits use, sharing, adaptation, distribution and reproduction in any medium or format, as long as you give appropriate credit to the original author(s) and the source, provide a link to the Creative Commons license and indicate if changes were made.

The images or other third party material in this chapter are included in the chapter's Creative Commons license, unless indicated otherwise in a credit line to the material. If material is not included in the chapter's Creative Commons license and your intended use is not permitted by statutory regulation or exceeds the permitted use, you will need to obtain permission directly from the copyright holder.

A Personal Story of 'Coincidence' in Becoming an Academic and Early Career Researcher: Being Creative to Push Boundaries

Anthony McKnight

This story that has been shared in a circular form, that is, not starting from a beginning nor finishing at an end, as I do not know exactly how I got here as an Early Career Researcher (ECR). This first-person reflection is how I would like to share, as when I first joined the education 'ranks' the main messages from my Aunties were, *sharing and caring*, plus *don't forget where you come from*. These statements from my Aunties are very important for me with one underlying meaning that came through overtime; don't forget all the living things and people that 'grew you up', family, Community, non-human Community and Country. Furthermore, don't get lost in the Western knowledge system while you are engaging within its power, processes and structures. I am continuously working on myself in regard to these comments and deepening my understanding of meaning. Therefore, these statements are always ringing in my ears! Thereby I would also like to pass on this message from my Aunties to the readers of this chapter. Thank you Aunties for indirectly passing on this pedagogy! Therefore, I have purposely written this short chapter that may be a bit confusing and not in an academic structure. Nevertheless, there is a flow of using memory, self-reflection and the possibility of what is next, without knowing, that is not always logical, to share a number of snapshots and teachings of my story traveling through academia. I hope you enjoy doing some of the work and finding something that works for you?

1 Always Remember to Share and Care Eh!

Just after I started my Ph.D. candidature journey, one of my Aunties came up to me on Country and said, *Eh, do you remember when a whole lot of families met at the velodrome when you were about 7ish?* I stood there for a while thinking back, and then said real

---

A. McKnight (✉)
University of Wollongong, Wollongong, NSW, Australia
e-mail: anthonym@uow.edu.au

© The Author(s) 2025
M. Trudgett et al. (eds.), *Indigenous Early Career Researchers in Australian Universities*, SpringerBriefs in Education,
https://doi.org/10.1007/978-981-97-2823-7_8

hesitantly, *I thiiinnnk so Aunty… it's a vague memory.'* Aunt continued to state within her own memory, which is pretty sharp, *Yeah me and couple of the other Aunties were watching you and said that one will become a teacher.* 'Oohh oookay' I said, trying really hard to remember that day.

By this time I had been working in the university sector for a number of years with a major focus on teaching pre-service teachers to implement and embed appropriate culturally informed approaches. In a way, at the time, I was only doing the Ph.D. to keep my job, because I love teaching education students preparing to teach our Aboriginal kids. However, the marking part is not such a good process culturally which creates more contestations between academia and our Aboriginal Knowledge systems. I really enjoy the challenge and providing opportunities for the preservice teachers to look at themselves and their own culture through Aboriginal pedagogies, thereby providing a platform to yarn and work together practically in finding new ways from old ways to enhance classroom practice when working through a Country centred approach. The next step I am learning within academia is being an Aboriginal ECR to place our pedagogical approaches, with permission, into research practice through Aboriginal methodologies.

2 Back to the Yarn with Aunty

I looked at Aunty who had been quiet for a while now, and I said to her, *Oohh yeah, that make sense to me now Aunty* as I was now sitting in my own memory, *that's why you did some of those things you did when I was younger.* Aunty just looked at me and smiled. I sometimes wondered when I was younger thinking to myself, *what was that all about, then shrugged my shoulders and carried on doing what I was doing,* typical young fella letting something just go over ya head eh! Or did it go over my head? This took me back further when I remembered listening to the mob talking about how the Old people use to observe and know a particular person's ability even when they were really young. Then indirectly the Old People would guide them in various ways to achieve this, in their own time. Then I had another realisation, *it wasn't just the Old people our Ancients, some of our Aunties and Uncles are still doing it today.* Cool eh! *Thanks Aunty,* I said, again she didn't look at me and had the smallest smile on her face without letting me know.

3 Flipping Back and Forth like a Memory

Before the above story occurred, I had only just gone back to working in the University system, as I left the sector about three years early, swearing I would never go back to a system full of toxicity and poison. However, in a way, I had no choice in the matter and found myself back teaching with a real sense of okay, you've put me back here Old fella's, so let's really make a difference for our kids in schools. To explain further, I had made my way back home, no job and needed to support my family, went for job at a university, didn't get it, but someone on the panel said a few weeks later, 'would you like to work in the School of Education?'. Yep, back in academia, something had to pay the bills at the time and now (is there a contradiction here?—sure is when two knowledge system contradicts). I invite you to sit with this statement.

Well back to the toxicity and focusing more on the Ph.D. and ECR story. I believe that the knowledge system we work in has a real poisonous element that affects many Aboriginal academics. In turn, non-Aboriginal academics suffer within the colonial venom as well. The colonial short cut learning, teaching and systematic approaches that focus on perfectionism, promotion and bringing in money for the university is quite damaging. Therefore, there is an ongoing story, with ups, downs, twists, tensions, confusion, and small successes as we may reluctantly compete, big note for promotion and play a game that is quite unhealthy in obtaining funding for research. However, after remembering that I liked teaching and the old fella's put me back in here, I said in my head 'okay let's try my very best to stay out of the poison' (hahahaha I can just hear my colleagues laughing). Thereby, to remain-sustain I had to take on 'doing' research and find an antidote at the same time.

4 Reminder, Back to the Start Through Aunties and Uncles Teaching

I had been involved in my candidature for about 8 months and one of my Uncles had come to the university to have a yarn with some of my students. After the seminar we had lunch and a cuppa and as I was walking him back to the car, I said to him, *I am not sure if I should be doing this Ph.D. thingy because...*, then I looked at him and said, *oh s*%#!*, in my mind. He stopped and Uncle's glare would have killed a buffalo from 100 metres away and he somewhat forcefully said, *You hold this f%#@&^#@ responsibility* and we started walking again, then he changed the topic to something else. *Message received Unk*, I said as I felt the lump on my head growing from the bundi. A number of years later, just before I sent off the hard copies of the Ph.D. to be marked, I went to Uncle's house and said, *I held my responsibility Unk!* Uncle just gave me a big smile that was followed by a big hug. Then that look of *'well ya better push some boundaries further now mate*. Again another messaged was received that was not said out load. Importantly and in respect I have to note, that this old fella had taught me patience and tolerance. Especially while working in this space of academia and life, but he also gave me a gift of how to respectfully 'push' (boundaries) things along and understand the way towards an antidote.

5 Another Teaching of Sharing and Caring: Gratitude

Importantly I must also be thankful towards a whole range of people and entities that guided me while doing a Ph.D. There are many other living things, family members and people that helped me along in this Ph.D. journey. A massive thank you to my wife and children who missed out on a lot while I was on the journey, again thank you so much. The Ph.D. and ECR journey is, and can be, very damaging to our self and mob. At the same time, this place can help give our voices a little bit more of an 'umph' in an education system that can't always hear, our voices. But every now and then they do, so at the moment, this is one thing that keeps me here in this space: how can we work with non-Aboriginal people/teachers to take care of Country and our children.

6 Going Back to the Start

I purposely started this story without telling people who I am, as I am that Aunty and the Uncle who guided me, in so many other ways, during my Ph.D. journey. To help clarify the meaning for the reader of the statement that *I am that Aunty or Uncle we come from the same branch,* we come from the same spirit or Ancestor, and this just doesn't have to mean bloodline, this is one form of many ways our people are connected through Country. I had to share my respects to them and others before you get to know me. ME is Mothers Entanglement, I am Awabakal, Gomaroi and hold Yuin, plus in not separating myself I am also of British Ancestry. What I have learnt as an ECR is you have to figure out a lot of things for yourself. On one level (culturally) that is a very good thing as you are not placing your responsibility onto someone else. However in a foreign but known system, a lot more support is required, but not in the sense of **entitlement**, which I can often see sneaking into this space of academia. The Old People and our Elders, not in this space of academia and in this space of academia, before us, did so much without entitlement and so can we if we want to walk alongside their footprints. Support in the Ph.D. and the ECR journey, I must admit does happen, but is often only through respectful relationship with our Aboriginal and non-Aboriginal colleagues. This support is often done voluntary because of a relationship that is reciprocal between colleagues. I would like to thank all of those people who have supported me plus ME (Mothers Entanglement) and for those that still are.

7 A Cryptic View

So is there an issue with the system? Well mainly yes and sometimes know! So I hope you enjoy my play with the English language to tell a story …!

> The system is a packet of 'Kettled Chips' not Kettle of fish,
> as fish can teach and nourish.
> The packet the separateness
> only opens for the Universities own advantage
> as we can be sealed and thrown in a box at any time.
> The box we have been kept in for a while now
> The kettle or the mess is what has happened in the past and now,
> to clean such a mess,
> it is often seen as complex, but is it?
> The answer has often been stated by many Aboriginal people
> and I would guess in this book as well,
> but more obviously Country is always providing us with the answers

Chips well is that us,

Aboriginal academics
plus some of our non-Aboriginal academic Sisters and Brothers
Are we starting to be recognised more often,
as people and knowledge custodians
who are worth engaging with
more readily and often
Is it only now we are worthwhile
^&%^$ me
Yep, had to get that out of my system,
but I cannot stay in anger,
a place where we as Aboriginal people have been forced to be for a long time
no longer please.
Back to the analogy,

that 'we' currently 'taste good'
or the flavour of the times
a comfortable or comfortable image
the packet of chips also
represents 'the Aboriginal bucket',
the funding,
that universities can dip their chips into
neoliberalist education
many of us are forced and may well be entrenched
the deep fryer.
Being flavoursome,

the knowledge
the sprinkling of the unique spices and condiments
the big hit
'Kettled chips'
Sweet Chilli and Sour Cream
replacing the Smiths
no I won't go there-here
not yet
But we do need to be opened,
taken out to nourish the system that compartmentalised us,
but not to be a consumable
The system consumes itself
And does need

knowledge that grounds people
instead of grounding people into the ground
This tension
is a very tricky place
as chips aren't seen as nourishing,
however yams are,
if seen in an appropriate light when shooting their spur
out of the ground.

So, the question is how can we support Aboriginal Knowledge and culture as people within a system well established in its own knowledge system? Well I don't have an answer, but we do, so we ask not to be placed in a packet in the first place and let us grow in our own ground as yams and find a place where non-Aboriginal people may want to be as well. I hope in your own mind and body you continue to engage in this representation with your own knowledge system to find connections with peoples' feelings and thoughts in this space: a craving to take care of Country. So let's push the boundaries. I hope you enjoyed unpacking the box and packet of this story in riddle in what you need. This is how many of our Old People in the past and today teach the children who will one day have the obligation and responsibility of taking care of Country in whatever space they find themselves. Country is still here where a university may well just sit on top!? Take care and remember to share. *Give it away to keep it* as that wonderful Old Fella use to say!

Dr. Anthony McKnight is an Awabakal, Gumaroi and Yuin Man. Anthony is a father, husband, uncle, son, grandson, brother, cousin, nephew, friend and cultural man. Anthony is currently a Senior Lecturer in the School of Education, Faculty of the Arts, Social Sciences and Humanities. Anthony respects Country and values the knowledge that has been taught to him from Country, Elders and teachers from community(s). He continuously and respectfully incorporates Aboriginal ways of knowing and learning, with a particular interest of contributing to placing Country centre to validate Aboriginal approaches in academia and schools. In 2017, Anthony completed a Ph.D. called *Singing Up Country in Academia: Teacher education academics and preservice teachers' experience with Yuin Country*. He holds a Master of Education (HRD) from the University of Sydney and a Bachelor of Education, Health and Physical Education from the University of Wollongong.

Open Access This chapter is licensed under the terms of the Creative Commons Attribution 4.0 International License (http://creativecommons.org/licenses/by/4.0/), which permits use, sharing, adaptation, distribution and reproduction in any medium or format, as long as you give appropriate credit to the original author(s) and the source, provide a link to the Creative Commons license and indicate if changes were made.

The images or other third party material in this chapter are included in the chapter's Creative Commons license, unless indicated otherwise in a credit line to the material. If material is not included in the chapter's Creative Commons license and your intended use is not permitted by statutory regulation or exceeds the permitted use, you will need to obtain permission directly from the copyright holder.

Yuwa Indigenous Early Career Researcher

Skye Akbar

I am a Waljen woman, Mum, Sister and Aunty. I work as a researcher and educator and my words here come from experiences in many work contexts and I write them hoping that they help you navigate a little easier, as Indigenous knowledges sharers past and present, helped me. Here are some words about my experience in academia so far: I am an early career researcher and here I describe some anecdotal generalised archetypes that I have encountered along the way. The experiences I have detailed here are not meant to be negative or positive- they just are. One of my biggest challenges has been that I have put so much energy in to trying to understand a system so foreign to me and my background that I have often been too busy trying to 'just keep swimming' that I have not noticed when something is fishy. I share these words in the hopes of making your pathway smoother.

1 The Token Blak

This is when you are the only one or one of only a few. The only one in your cohort, the only one at your discipline event, the only one in your university etc. Management may be super supportive, but the reality is that your existence and your requirement to meet the same performance indicators as other academics will uncover issues that no one previously noticed. Perhaps it turns out some of the staff are a little racisty? Perhaps some of the structural pathways for key job requirements are culturally biased? Perhaps management think that they are helping when in fact they are making you a target for predatory academics? Either way, these problems may have been unnoticed before and you are going to be forced into a position required

S. Akbar (✉)
University of South Australia, Adelaide, Australia
e-mail: skye.akbar@unisa.edu

© The Author(s) 2025
M. Trudgett et al. (eds.), *Indigenous Early Career Researchers in Australian Universities*, SpringerBriefs in Education,
https://doi.org/10.1007/978-981-97-2823-7_9

to identify, articulate and raise very prickly issues, often from a very unpowerful career position. This can make others see you as ill fitting, not a team player, or a complainer. It's a trope, but look to Community for guidance, choose your battles, and practice self-care.

2 Being the Other

For a long time some non-Indigenous academics have made a career path from researching Indigenous themes and issues. In funding applications, you may notice phrases like: 'My work will support Indigenous people to do better', or something similar. Some of these academics mean it and some do not. Some will take issue with no longer leading in this space and may feel threatened by the existence of an Indigenous researcher and make overt or covert plans to neutralise their threat. Notice who has long term productive relationships with Indigenous scholars and who truthfully anticipates, acknowledges, monitors and reports impacts on Community resulting from their research, and who does not.

3 The Bullied

Some academics are bullies; it is a relentless industry that can bring out the best and worst in people. Not all the bullies are non-Indigenous. The line between being held to account by Community, and academic bullying, is difficult to identify when the diversity of our nation's cultures is amalgamated to suit the institution. This is one of the trickiest contexts to navigate and a talk with your Community will always help shed light.

4 The Pull

Once people are aware of your existence and identity they will be presenting you with many opportunities. An important aspect of academia is picking your path, your knowledge and expertise and growing this area deeply. Due to The Pull you will be lured in many directions and many opportunities come with a smiling face, saying 'I'm here to help you'. But following each of these pathways even just a little is time and energy away from the pathway that grows your contribution and supports your Community. Learn where you add most value, and know your own goal, which may be different to the non-Indigenous researchers and the institution.

5 The Sell

Predatory academics will see you, and the potential for networks and funding, as a dollar sign. Some may seek out high value research relationships and use your position within the Community and university as a bargaining chip to improve their chances of getting a foot in the door with clients and funders. Some may misrepresent your qualifications away from your key work or discipline to match their needs with a third party. Some may position your existence as an answer to the deficit thinking in their worldview. You may or may not be aware that they are doing this, which makes it harder to fight against it. Again, talk to your people, know your own goal and practice the many ways to say no.

6 The Culture Against You

This is when an academic knowing of Indigenous culture will use cultural elements to attempt to pressure you to do what they want. They may say that if you don't agree to be listed on their grant you are limiting the opportunities for you to help the Community. They may lament to you that they do not want to pressure younger Indigenous researchers and so could you just agree to do a little on the project so you can be a named applicant on their grant. They may say that they won't need much of your time but it'd be good to have some cultural oversight so you'll need to be listed as a Lead Researcher. This is a particularly tricky situation because these practitioners are very good at manipulating and it is difficult to get away from them because they are highly motivated to use their knowledge of culture to their advantage.

7 The Representative

You may be the first, the only, or one of a few Indigenous academics. Some in academia are aware that systematic exclusion of groups has led to a lack of diversity and that this impacts their genuine aspirations and ability to make inclusive pathways, policy and decisions. This has led to the acknowledgment of the positive impact of representation of diversity on groups, committees, boards and thinking in general as they need us, specifically our brains and narratives of lived experience. You may receive invitations to participate in groups, boards and committees for all manner of things and some of those will include very high-level people and positions. Given the complexity of academic institutions it can be difficult to understand what is an opportunity and what is laborious. Try to identify where you can contribute the most and what motivates you.

8 The Report

Institutions are required to report on aspects of 'Indigenous engagement'. You are a reportable 'Indigenous engagement'. Areas of the institution that you previously didn't know existed may ask for information and data for reports you didn't know existed. The requests will come from wide and far and will use your time and energy as you have to self-educate on what on earth these requests require of you and if it is a part of your job to do this work and if it's in your interest to associate yourself with the requester and the requester's agenda.

9 The Helping Out

Requests to 'help out' may come with advice of good exposure or experience. While initially I accepted these types of roles because I am an inherent people pleaser who had no idea what I was doing, I came to realise that every time I helped someone for free I take the work from an Indigenous person who would have asked to have been paid for that task. So I now try to direct people to someone either already being paid to help in that type of task or someone who puts dinner on their table by doing that type of work. Similarly, when I engage Indigenous businesspeople if they ask for less than the industry standard cost for a task, I tell them they need to rethink their quote to align with industry standard.

10 The Over Sell and Under Deliver

Your institution may have a collection of documents that say how they will support Indigenous people, researchers, communities and research themes. Know that while there may be good intentions there are sometimes challenges in operationalisation. This is possibly because academia is one umbrella term given to eleventy-million different types of activity and management may not be aware of all of the activities required of a researcher who walk in Two Worlds and are accountable to Community in their heart and to academia for the cost of living. Being expected to represent Community and do the same job as everyone else by your institution means you will work two times as hard for one times the remuneration. While announcements are made at federal, state and institutional level about seemingly great initiatives, the application throughout the research and teaching process may not have been thought through and some tricky areas to navigate may arise with no one having ever thought through that this problem would inevitably impact you.

11 The Indigenous Researcher as a Teacher

Many areas of institutions are looking to have an Indigenous person teach about Indigenous issues. For many, this means teaching a general cohort of students, mostly non-Indigenous people, some only there because the course is mandatory. Sadly, given the culture of Australia, this means that you may face racism, stereotyping and inappropriate challenges from students in class and in assessments. This raises concerns for educators working in an environment where student evaluation of teaching informs activities like probation and promotion. It also means that your teaching will take a level of personal energy and engagement unlike others. Choosing to insert narratives of your own experiences of policy instigated intergenerational traumas will make students listen more keenly as they hear firsthand of Indigenous experiences, but it will leave you exhausted in a way that other academics are not.

12 The Publication Gauntlet

Journals may state scopes and aims that include interest in minority and Indigenous issues but that does not always mean they will include work by academics from minority and Indigenous backgrounds. Journals and reviewers, given the historical demographics of academia, may not understand your work or may be familiar with Indigenous people only in theory and this may be reflected in the double-blind peer review process. But if non-Indigenous people were capable of the same type and level of work as a researcher who is Indigenous we wouldn't need Indigenous researchers to research Indigenous issues in the way that we do. Your contribution is unique and valuable. Publications last forever so make your narrative strengths based and target the audience important to you.

13 The Proper Way or the Quick Way

When management are announcing the importance of researching Indigenous issues they often skip over how difficult it is. Yes, there is opportunity to make a difference and support positive change when researching issues impacting Indigenous peoples. But, in addition to the other hurdles, perhaps you'll not find the literature you need taught in mainstream courses, you'll not find the methodologies you're likely to require commonly practiced and taught at your institution. Perhaps you are likely to find you need to do all the additional work to locate your research issue and context within academic discourse because an Indigenous perspective has not been included before. The approvals and reporting may be strenuous and there may be additional processes and committees and groups you need to go through to undertake your research. While this is challenging and exhausting to do once, over the course of a few years you are looking at significant setbacks in comparison to academics who write non evidence-based work, use secondary data, or research only non-Indigenous issues. You may gain an enormous body of experience in a short amount of time but this may not be reflected in the types of outputs that advance your career. Time and energy are finite and the learning curve is steep.

14 The Employment Gap

In the desperate situation when an institution has trouble recruiting and retaining staff there are people who can justify to themselves asking Indigenous staff to take on tasks they are not experienced, qualified, time allocated, acknowledged or ready for. This is the mainstream academy putting pressure on Indigenous researchers to make up for the 'employment gap' and weaponizing their incompetence. This leads to Indigenous people being in roles they are not yet ready to do, that feel overwhelming and that can overshadow the work that will lead them to a quality track record. It also leads to fellow Indigenous employees being uncomfortable as they watch people with less experience and qualifications being promoted past them because they know that person is saying yes to opportunities for which they are not qualified or experienced. In these contexts, you'll need to decide if you want fast promotions or a meaningful steady journey.

15 The 'New to This Space' Researcher

As the pressure on academics increases more academics are looking for alternate places to find funding. This leads to academics who have not previously worked in the space of Indigenous research to think about giving it a go. Often influenced by a recent management speech or initiative announcement, they may approach you from any angle with the phrase 'Can I buy you a coffee' featuring in their initial contact. They are seeking a Subject Matter Expert, and while that's all good, they may have made no previous effort to learn about research in this context. They may have never heard of Australian Institute of Aboriginal and Torres Strait Islander Studies (AIATSIS), or considered the ethical implications of their ideas for Indigenous Communities, and the challenge is that it's left up to you to identify whether this person is experienced, inexperienced but willing to make a long term investment and appropriate for this space, or if you've wasted another hour of your limited time in exchange for one coffee.

16 A Note, for Now…

Recently I realised that while I am trying hard to enact and support change from within academia, I may be unlikely to actually see the impact of those changes, as I now realise the many strong Indigenous researchers before me may have also found.

In my life I am grateful for my strong Community and in my career I have been grateful to know amazing Indigenous scholars. I am proud of my people. I feel that our presence in academia enables us to define what success, and knowledge, is to us in our own ways, albeit within this colonial institution.

The thing is, what I have written here, I am confident it is not exceptional, and that is why I have written it down. From speaking to my fellow Indigenous researchers I know that these challenges I have faced are not unique, many aspects of this text represent an all too often shared experience amongst a group of outliers—Indigenous people who participate in colonial institutions. Despite these challenges being common, the Indigenous academics that I know are incredibly Community orientated, interesting, and passionate people and I know each of them makes our world a better place. So here is what I am going to try: I am going to do my best for as long as I can and leave the door ajar for you and hope that you can wedge it open just that little bit further for the next of us.

Best of luck,
Dr Skye Akbar

Dr. Skye Akbar is a Waljen woman, a mum, sister and aunty. As a researcher and educator her interests are Aboriginal business research, regional business research, research methods and ethics, community life, culturally informed local solutions and evidence-based decision making.

Open Access This chapter is licensed under the terms of the Creative Commons Attribution 4.0 International License (http://creativecommons.org/licenses/by/4.0/), which permits use, sharing, adaptation, distribution and reproduction in any medium or format, as long as you give appropriate credit to the original author(s) and the source, provide a link to the Creative Commons license and indicate if changes were made.

The images or other third party material in this chapter are included in the chapter's Creative Commons license, unless indicated otherwise in a credit line to the material. If material is not included in the chapter's Creative Commons license and your intended use is not permitted by statutory regulation or exceeds the permitted use, you will need to obtain permission directly from the copyright holder.

A Swim in the Rough Surf—Deaf, Aboriginal, and at the Biggest School of All

Scott Avery

This one is for the young fella with dead ears. You don't see many of us around, so you might think that you are out there on your own. But there are others like you that are here now, and have been here before you, hidden in plain sight, and have a story much like yours. You just need to know where to look.

The town clinic will talk to and your family and your teachers and say that you 'suffer' from something they will call hearing 'loss'. You don't understand what it is you have lost, as it has been that way for you as long as you can remember. Some of the doctors at the clinic will talk about your 'good ear' and 'bad ear'. This is also strange thing for you to understand as your ears aren't gammin or bad, they are just dead.

The town clinic will say that they can fix you like they can fix a broken toy. Eventually, they give you a machine to put on your ears. They look like trinkets, but they will give you a superpower so you can hear the noise. The town clinic will be very proud of what they have given you. Your family will be excited and sad at the same time.

Healing man tells you the story of the old way. They say that the quiet is your natural world and how it is meant to be. You do not suffer anything or need to be fixed. The town people only started thinking that dead-eared people needed fixing

---

S. Avery (✉)
University of Technology Sydney, Sydney, NSW, Australia
e-mail: scott.avery@uts.edu.au

© The Author(s) 2025
M. Trudgett et al. (eds.), *Indigenous Early Career Researchers in Australian Universities*, SpringerBriefs in Education,
https://doi.org/10.1007/978-981-97-2823-7_10

since the boats with the white sails landed on the shore. The old way of your peoples is how nature intends it to be. They remind you that you can take your trinkets off and go to a quiet place that no one else can know of. This is the real superpower, the one that only you can own.

Some connect through the land, but you connect through the sea. The sea has no need for sound, so it is your place of peace.

You have been in the pond and the river before, but now you want to take on the biggest ocean. Getting into the big ocean will be hard as there is a big fence in the way. The front gates are locked by the time you get there, but you can find a hole in the fence a bit further down. You may have to walk a bit further than most, but not near as far as it is for others, and then there are the ones who won't be able to get in at all. There are people already inside who know of this way in and can guide you through. Just don't make too much noise until you are well and truly inside.

One of the first things you will see once you are inside is the tight group standing in their circle. You will know them by their colours that they wear. The ones who know you from your community will shout out for you join them. You look around but can't find another dead-eared person to stand beside, so the swim will be yours and yours alone. But it gives you comfort to know that everyone in the circle has their own path that they are following, and that they will have your back when you head out.

The people guarding the waterline will tell you where you must swim and what style you must use. They will tell you to stay close to shore where they can save you. Look at the people that have won prizes and do as they do, they will say. But it is very crowded and there are lots of people swimming over the top of each other, so the best you can do here is splash around.

Healing man has told you of a different place. It is a place known by the old ways, and it hasn't been written down. It will be much harder for you here but will make for a grand adventure. So this is where you choose to swim.

It is calm at first, and tricks you into thinking it might be easier than you first thought. Then the further you go out, the struggle comes. The waves come at you from different directions. You can see the big waves from the front, and knowing they are coming, you can dive deep. Then when you come up, waves will hit you from the side and you take in the water. The current will drag you towards the rocks. You start to fight it, but then you come to accept that the sea is just doing what it is made to do. Healing man has told you that just as you are about to hit the rocks, the current will turn and take you from it. So you swim with it, the only way out is to keep going in.

As you swim from the headland, you watch out for the sharks. Aunt has told you with a smile on her face that sharks don't go for black fellas. She is right so far. You never feel completely safe but deep down you know the ocean is their home and you learn to respect that. It's the stingers that you need to watchful of. The beautiful looking ones will lure you towards them, and those are the ones that will hurt you the most.

There will come a point beyond the break when the seas will calm. Here, you are in your place, and all you can hear is the imagined sounds of the water slushing through seashells. Away from the shouting on the shoreline, the only thing that you hear is that you are deaf and of the old way, and you can be proud of both.

You watch as the sun, the giver of life, calmly sets itself down as it did yesterday and will again tomorrow. You can see your celestial teachers signal to you that you are who you are and where you are for a reason, and it's going to be ok.

Acknowledgement

I honour the Elders, people with disability, scholars, and educators for their wisdom and knowledge shared generously, both in published and unwritten forms, that has shaped how I now see the world.

1 Author's Guide to Critical Interpretation

(This one is for the hearing and the abled).

I am profoundly deaf and of the Worimi people, proud times two, and entered University as an academic in 2020 following the completion of my Ph.D. the year prior. My Ph.D. in Indigenous disability and inclusion was completed during a decade's worth of systemic advocacy at the First Peoples Disability Network, a community-governed Indigenous Disability Peoples Organisation, a comparatively tiny organisation compared to a university but one nonetheless that punches well above its weight division. The cultural contrast on what is valued and how things are done in 'community' compared to 'university' brings an understated third dimension to my 'positionality' (Nakata, 2007), adding to being deaf and Aboriginal.

My entry into academia was enabled through my University's Indigenous employment strategy, one of many of the Indigenous support networks that are well ensconced in the sector. The number of respected Aboriginal and Torres Strait Islander Professors and academics, their high visibility in leadership positions, the Indigenous student support units, the staff networks and events, have all have created a sense that as an Aboriginal academic I belong in a university. Then I look around and ask, where are all the deaf people?

The intersection of Indigenous and disability research is positioned as a narrow niche within the two larger social research agendas. In a room of disability researchers, you are the one in the room that is talking about structural racism; in a room of Indigenous researchers, you are the one that is talking about structural ableism. It is rare that the compounding effect of structural ableism and structural racism is dedicated topic of discussion in either of these rooms. This experience is like being everyone's second favourite football team. Everyone wants you to do well, but they have their own team to barrack for so no one buys the jersey. There is an upside of being affiliated within both the Indigenous and the disability community is that you tick two diversity boxes for the price of one, which means you end up receiving lots of invites to add your as name as an annexe to someone else's agenda.

Discovering Crenshaw's theorisation of 'intersectionality' (Crenshaw, 1991) was something of a revelation, both personally and for the First Nations disability community. 'Intersectionality' has given the vocabulary through which to express the frustrations of being subjected to the dual forces of structural racism and structural ableism (at least) that drives the social marginalisation of people with our community. Within the academy, 'intersectionality' is not something that attached to any individual academic or researcher; but it does attach itself to the cause, and the type of community centred Indigenous disability research is very much situated at the outskirts of what is viewed as accepted research.

There is an increasing body of literature and research on institutionalised racism within the academy by other Indigenous scholars that will do far better that I in explain and exposing it, and there are platforms available for it. However, the deaf and disability experience within scholarship remains a great unspoken. Part of this is the nature of ableist discrimination that involves the phenomena of 'othering' (Mik-Meyer, 2016). Whereas experiences of racism involve a conflict—you have a right to speak and there are platforms for you to do so, but you risk being attached for it. With ableist discrimination, you are not even in the room. A differentiating aspect of ableist discrimination to other forms of discrimination is a tacit presumption that people with disability do not have the capacity to speak for themselves in the first place.

This why the glamour that is afforded to medical and scientific models of research can be confronting to some people within the disability community. The dominant narrative of a medical model of research is that deaf and disabled people are broken and can be fixed by the latest research innovation. The values and ethics of what and how this research is conducted is not determined by disability community but through intermediaries—the scientists, the service providers, the carers, the trustees—all supported by an array of academic rituals that are designed to keep the deaf and disabled under the microscope and safely within the petri dish.

The institutionalised ableism within the academy is merely an extension of the ableism that occurs within the society more generally. Outside the academy, I have had to complete 'hearing handicap audits' which asked, 'how handicapped are you by your hearing loss?' Within the academy, I have had to respond to a health and medical ethics committee directives that suggested I need additional procedures to determine whether deaf people I wished to interview had the capacity to participate in research (Avery, 2019). The nature of ableism silences these experiences of deaf and disabled people within the academy, and there has not been enough conscious enquiry to know the extent to which others have been impacted by similar experiences. Tackling ableism within the learning world is the next frontier for those aspiring to educational justice.

Being closely connected to an Indigenous disability community and having your skin in the game is strangely liberating, as you have no option but do what your community asks and expects of you. My community of belonging, the First Nations disability community, does not honour the accolades, it honours the struggle. This has been the way of the Elders and leaders who have shared their wisdom to this generation of scholars (Bostock, 1991), which in turn will be handed down to future generations. So turn up we have, and turn up we shall. We do this because we know somewhere in Australia right now there is a young deaf Aboriginal person sitting in a classroom battling it out, who needs to see, hear and know that despite what they think that they face in front of them, if they look to the clues handed out in the biggest school of all, then they can survive it, and that it is going to be ok.

Professor Scott Avery

References

Avery, S. (2019). *'We go hunting together':Cultural and community inclusion as a moderator of social inequality experienced by Aboriginal and Torres Strait Islander people with disability.* University of Technology Sydney.

Bostock, L. (1991). Access and equity for people with a double disadvantage. *Australian Disability Review, 1*(2), 3–8.

Crenshaw, K. (1991). Mapping the margins: Intersectionality, identity politics, and violence against women of color. *Stanford Law Review, 43*(6), 1241–1299.

Mik-Mayer, N. (2016). Othering, ableism and disability: A discursive analysis of co-workers' construction of colleagues with visible impairments. *Human Relations, 69*(6), 1341–1363.

Nakata, M. (2007) *Disciplining the savages: Savaging the disciplines.* Aboriginal Studies Press.

Professor Scott Avery is an Indigenous researcher who is profoundly deaf. He developed his interest and approach to disability and inclusion research whilst working in community roles in the Australian Indigenous disability community, where he maintains a close connection with the First Peoples Disability Network. He has authored the book 'Culture is Inclusion: A narrative of Aboriginal and Torres Strait Islander peoples with disability' (2018) based on his research. He has extensive experience in conducting community-based research and policy in Indigenous and disability organisations and has been appointed as an expert advisor to numerous government bodies.

Open Access This chapter is licensed under the terms of the Creative Commons Attribution 4.0 International License (http://creativecommons.org/licenses/by/4.0/), which permits use, sharing, adaptation, distribution and reproduction in any medium or format, as long as you give appropriate credit to the original author(s) and the source, provide a link to the Creative Commons license and indicate if changes were made.

The images or other third party material in this chapter are included in the chapter's Creative Commons license, unless indicated otherwise in a credit line to the material. If material is not included in the chapter's Creative Commons license and your intended use is not permitted by statutory regulation or exceeds the permitted use, you will need to obtain permission directly from the copyright holder.

Lessons Along the Way—8 Rules for Surviving Academia as an Aboriginal Early Career Researcher

BJ Newton

I have been asked to contribute a chapter to this book sharing my experiences as an Aboriginal Early Career Researcher. I write this chapter from the heart, as a gift for fellow Aboriginal colleagues in the academic space and I hope you find value in the insights I am about to share.

I am a Wiradjuri woman based at the University of New South Wales Sydney on Bidjigal land. My background is in social work and sociology, and I completed my Ph.D. at UNSW at the end of 2016. I have been working as a researcher for well over a decade, mostly on evaluations and commissioned projects in child protection, and domestic and family violence research. Post-doctorate, I have been focusing my energy on my own research and am leading an Australian Research Council (ARC) Discovery Indigenous grant, called *Bring them home keep them home*, exploring successful pathways to child restoration for Aboriginal children from out-of-home care. I also have two ARC Linkage grants. From 2021 I found myself quite unexpectedly in a leadership role in my faculty when I was appointed as the inaugural Associate Dean Indigenous. In this leadership position I had to contend with trading off my time and energy doing faculty change-making as opposed to focusing all my attention on contributing to social change through my research. Half-way through 2022, while writing this chapter, I decided to step down from this role to prioritise what I am most passionate about: using research as the mechanism to influence child protection policy and practice.

In this chapter, I share some of the strategies I have learned during my time working in academia, to successfully navigate the institution. I am calling these my *Rules for Surviving Academia as an Aboriginal Early Career Researcher*. A few caveats before reading on. These rules are only based on my experience working in one institution, and the context may look very different in other universities.

BJ Newton (✉)
UNSW Sydney, Sydney, NSW, Australia
e-mail: b.newton@unsw.edu.au

© The Author(s) 2025
M. Trudgett et al. (eds.), *Indigenous Early Career Researchers in Australian Universities*, SpringerBriefs in Education,
https://doi.org/10.1007/978-981-97-2823-7_11

Similarly, I have worked most of my career in a research-only role and have not had to negotiate the challenges of a teaching load. Finally, I am still learning and know there are many more experiences ahead to further shape my thinking about this topic. So, this list of rules is by no means comprehensive, and I encourage others to seek opportunities to add to our collective experience and knowledges by sharing their own rules for surviving academia.

1 Rule 1: Know Your Values

The three key interrelated values fundamental in all the work that I do are integrity, accountability, and autonomy. I will not compromise my cultural, ethical, or moral integrity under any circumstances. At times this can be at conflict with decisions which could surely further my career or promotion opportunities, however for me doing what is right will always trump doing what leads to settler colonial measures of success or status; I am in academia to influence social change and justice for Aboriginal peoples first and foremost.

This feeds into the value of accountability. As Aboriginal academics we are always accountable to our mobs and to the communities and organisations we serve through our research. Grounding myself through an acute awareness of my accountabilities to those impacted by the work that I do, whether in research, teaching, or university leadership, ensures that social justice and equity for Aboriginal peoples is always front and centre of all decisions I make and projects I pursue.

Which leads to the third value of autonomy, the backbone of the other two values. If I don't feel as though I am autonomous in my work, then it will be difficult to honour the other values of integrity and accountability. Feeling autonomous in academia can be challenging, particularly for emerging scholars, however it is necessary to have both a fulfilling and meaningful academic career. The following rules will provide insight into how you can achieve autonomy as an early career academic.

2 Rule 2: Create a Culturally Safe Environment for Yourself

In research, the nature of research funding and pressures to secure competitive grants breeds epistemic violence for Aboriginal researchers who are often pulled onto multiple projects to fulfil the role of 'Aboriginal researcher' as required by their funding conditions. We can feel trapped or obligated to be named on *just one more* project, and if we do apologetically refuse because we are too overloaded, then we are to blame because there aren't enough Aboriginal researchers to do the work and therefore each project relies on us to be that token.

Aboriginal researchers can often feel pressured to do the community engagement work. This places us in a difficult position because we don't want to compromise our reputation, relationships with community, and potentially causing harm or at the very least, subjecting other Aboriginal peoples to research that has no benefits and may exploit and stigmatise Aboriginal peoples further.

In the teaching space, my limited experience convening one class impacted me so greatly that I wrote a paper about cultural safety in the classroom (Newton, 2021). In a nutshell, I discuss the four strategies that emerged organically for me to create a culturally safe environment while I was teaching a core social work course focused on working with Aboriginal peoples, and thus, sustain me in this role:

1. Protecting my story- This was key to reducing my sense of feeling vulnerable and objectified as the only Aboriginal person in the lecture theatre
2. Respecting and normalising the diversity of identity- All 100 + students in that cohort did not identify as Aboriginal or Torres Strait Islander and many had very little understanding of Aboriginal cultures, so spending the time unpacking the diversity of First Nations peoples across the country was critical
3. Collaborative and respectful learning- We created an open, non-judgemental, and supportive learning environment, based on mutual respect and a commitment to embracing the experience without guilt or shame
4. Minimising the risk of experiencing trauma from content- Much of the course content can trigger distress and trauma, and I mitigated this through sharing the lecturing load to distance myself for a couple of weeks and drawing on support from my trusted colleagues and friends.

3 Rule 3: Pursue Your Own Research

Some academics think as Aboriginal researchers, we risk being pigeonholed in the role of the Aboriginal researcher on the team, destined to work for the research priorities of others, carrying out community engagement and lending cultural knowledge and expertise to project after project without the opportunity to pursue our own interests, and indeed, excel in academia. I don't think this concern is unfounded; this could and does certainly happen when Aboriginal academics are overloaded with service responsibilities (above and beyond non-Aboriginal people), teaching and/or commissioned research to the degree that they have no capacity to pursue their own career goals.

I remember being approached by a colleague to collaborate on an Australian Research Council project. This colleague told me a cautionary story about an Aboriginal academic they once knew that was never promoted beyond the lecturer level, because they never had the opportunity to be a chief investigator in the projects they worked on. This colleague pitched to me, that they were giving me the opportunity to work on a project as a chief investigator and I needed this/their research to move up in the world of academia. This conversation came from a place of good intentions, but at the same time was incredibly patronizing and condescending, as if I couldn't progress on my own and needed the support of this colleague to do so. This was a stark reminder of my relegated place in the institution; that I will always be perceived as the *Aboriginal* researcher, with a discreet expertise, used for the purposes of bolstering the Indigenous credibility of projects led by non-Aboriginal researchers- unless I did something about it. That conversation planted the seed for my determination to do my own research on my own terms.

My advice to other Aboriginal researchers would be to carve out a place for yourself in research and knowledge generation by pursuing your own research. Apply for grants that will enable you the autonomy to do research that is meaningful to you and that progresses the interests and priorities of stakeholders in your research.

4 Rule 4: Harness the Power of the Collective Voice

Advocacy within institutions is very similar to advocacy in other settings, which many of us are familiar with through our personal and professional experiences. The more people drawing attention to the inequities and shortfalls of the institution for Aboriginal staff and students, the more likely leaders in decision-making positions will listen. It is important to identify and recruit genuine and trustworthy allies who will support you in your institutional advocacy, know when to step back and respect your leaderships in this space, and when to take some of the burden of the institutional load off your shoulders.

It is imperative that you support your Aboriginal colleagues and know that they support you. This doesn't mean you all need to agree on all matters, but there needs to be a mutual respect and understanding that you are working for the same cause, and divisions between Aboriginal staff members only serves to further the interests of the institution, and at the expense of our own.

5 Rule 5: Identify Genuine and Trustworthy Leaders to Support Your Cause

Without the support and advocacy of more senior colleagues and leaders, it will be very difficult to make changes within the institution. Leaders have a significant impact on workplace culture and the likelihood of change being implemented and sustained. Enlist the support of influential colleagues to help amplify the needs of Aboriginal staff and students in the institution. If my Dean (and the Acting Dean before her) was not genuinely committed to Indigenous equity and embedding Indigenous priorities and interests as core functioning across the faculty, very little change would be realised, least of which the establishment of Indigenous leadership (my Associate Dean role) at the faculty level.

6 Rule 6: Understand the University System to Drive Your Own Career Progression

This one is very important, though not something you are explicitly taught as an emerging scholar. It is imperative that you spend time talking with your mentors, Ph.D. supervisors, and senior colleagues about how the university system works. A few years ago, I did not know anything about the university hierarchy, or how all the different divisions and faculties worked together. I had a limited understanding of competitive research funding streams, or publication hierarchies and how these impacted on your case for promotion.

Once you start funding your own research, you will be in a position to build your autonomy as an academic (see Rule 1): buy-out your teaching or commissioned research time, choose the research projects you will work on, pursue voluntary or service roles that speak to your interests, and use your voice and authority to influence change at multiple touch points, both internal and external to the institution.

7 Rule 7: Leverage Your Position to Make Change

As Aboriginal academics, we are cognisant of walking within an institutional system that carries, and in many ways, continues the legacy of Indigenous oppression and inequity. That said, there has never been a more opportune time for Aboriginal people to pursue a career in academia, and in a way that we can remain true to our values.

Aboriginal research is a high priority for funders, and in the cut-throat world of competitive grants the truth is that having an Aboriginal researcher and indeed, an Aboriginal-focus or component in your research can in many instances give you a competitive edge; this can be very dangerous to Aboriginal researchers, and importantly, Aboriginal Communities if the research team is ingenuine and inexperienced in Indigenous research methods and principles (on a side note, this raises the necessity for Aboriginal ethics boards). However, we can use this to our advantage. As Aboriginal researchers we are in high-demand, and even junior researchers can use this both to the benefit of highlighting the research needs of Aboriginal peoples and communities, and as leverage to be unwavering in our approach to conducting research that follows Aboriginal ethics principles and that advocates for social change.

In teaching, increasingly academic qualifications require graduates to demonstrate an understanding of Indigenous knowledges and the impact of colonisation, as disciplines increasingly engage in the process of decolonising curricula and teaching students about their own biases and positionality against the backdrop of invaded sovereign Indigenous nations. This need calls for Aboriginal academics to take the lead; it is an opportunity for us to advocate for what we need to support and sustain us in our roles, and for what we know is essential for our cultural integrity (see Rule 1). We can leverage this need to influence our schools, faculties and wider institutions to invest in recruiting more Aboriginal people to the university, and to appoint local and appropriate Aboriginal leaders and knowledge holders to positions that recognise their expertise in Indigenous education.

As Associate Dean, I used my position to implement significant changes to directly support and improve the equity and experiences of Aboriginal staff and students and influence a cultural shift at the faculty level. This was by no means easy, and I have some key insights to share. Pursuing Indigenous equity and goals requires much more than commitment from leadership and goodwill of colleagues. For change to be implemented and sustainable, the institution also needs to demonstrate that commitment by allocating adequate resourcing and infrastructure so that we can do the work that needs to be done. Anything else is just token lip service (and covert institutional racism) and creates more pressure for Aboriginal staff tasked with leading this change. Despite this, I am proud of my achievements as Associate Dean.

8   Rule 8: Know Your Priorities

From an ECR perspective I have sacrificed a critical time in my post-doctorate window to undertake the Associate Dean role; university leadership is extremely administrative heavy and carries a significant mental load that inevitably takes you away from your research and in turn, your capacity to publish. These are key considerations for any academic, but particularly ECRs when considering positions that will impact your research. Coming out the other side of a leadership position, my priorities are clear. I don't know what the future holds for me in academia, but what I do know is that following the rules described in this chapter has helped see me through this far.

Dr. BJ Newton is a proud Wiradjuri woman and mother to three young children. BJ is a Senior Research Fellow at the Social Policy Research Centre within UNSW Sydney. She specialises in Indigenous research methods and child protection research and policy. Her research focuses on working in partnership with Aboriginal organisations to build evidence and support Aboriginal families interfacing with child protection systems. BJ was the inaugural Associate Dean (Indigenous) of the Faculty of Arts, Design and Architecture, a position which she held between Jan 2021–Aug 2022. BJ then transitioned from this role to take up a prestigious Scientia Fellowship which enables her to focus on research.

Open Access This chapter is licensed under the terms of the Creative Commons Attribution 4.0 International License (http://creativecommons.org/licenses/by/4.0/), which permits use, sharing, adaptation, distribution and reproduction in any medium or format, as long as you give appropriate credit to the original author(s) and the source, provide a link to the Creative Commons license and indicate if changes were made.

The images or other third party material in this chapter are included in the chapter's Creative Commons license, unless indicated otherwise in a credit line to the material. If material is not included in the chapter's Creative Commons license and your intended use is not permitted by statutory regulation or exceeds the permitted use, you will need to obtain permission directly from the copyright holder.

Aspirations

Mentoring Our Way for the Future of Indigenous Scholarship

Tristan Kennedy

1 Introduction

I am a Noongar Australian. I grew up on Kaurna Country in South Australia and currently work on the unceded sovereign lands of the Wallamattagal people of the Dharug Nation. I have worked and studied at two higher education institutions in Australia. In both workplaces I have built my academic career in collaboration and with support from colleagues and community members. I have embraced and valued meaningful, mostly informal, mentorship since becoming an Early Career Researcher. There has been no greater support for my professional development than that which I gained through mentorship from established Indigenous scholars within well connected, community focussed workplaces.

The connections that Indigenous scholars create and maintain with our communities are truly unique in academia. Nakata (2006) identifies the inseparability of Indigenous academic work and the commitment to 'rebuilding Indigenous communities and futures' (p. 266): that is, to conduct research that is relevant and beneficial to our communities and to work in ways that build the capacity of the next generation of Indigenous scholars. Having worked and studied within and outside Indigenous departments and Indigenous support units, my experience is that Indigenous academics are far more likely to offer cultural support and advice amongst colleagues, to teach and research collaboratively, and to include the wider community of knowledge holders in the process of knowledge formation.

One of the core commitments made by Indigenous scholars is to promote and support up and coming scholars of the future. Mentorship in the spirit of 'growing our own' is a core scholarly value of one of my mentors, Professor Bronwyn Carlson. Paying forward to junior Indigenous scholars for the future of Indigenous

---

T. Kennedy (✉)
Monash University, Clayton, VIC, Australia
e-mail: Tristan.kennedy@monash.edu

research and scholarship is something which I embrace as my core responsibility to Australian and global Indigenous communities. I value the knowledge and skills I have developed through the opportunities provided to me by mentors across my time in academia. I intend that my teaching, research, and community service will remain centred on paying forward to the next generation of Indigenous scholars.

2 Mentoring in the Academy

Much has been written about mentoring in higher education in Australia and the world. The focus of much of this work tends toward areas where mentorship is seen as part of the process of gaining professional registration. For instance, in medical and educational degree programs there exists an industry expectation that students, pre-registration, undergo 'blocks' or periods of mentoring and practice under the supervision of already qualified professionals. Krishna et al. (2020) discuss the importance of mentoring in preparing medical students to enter a field where lives depend upon them being able to handle the rigours of the job. Of course, as academics working outside hospital emergency departments, the stakes are different. Mentoring in academia is seen not as a pre-requisite for career development but a positive collaborative effort to build knowledge, skills, and importantly publication track records. Focusing specifically on the experiences of academics, Ambler et al. (2016) found that participants noted the benefits of mentoring as establishing friendships and further career advancement. They also noted that mentoring relationships had the potential to create 'feelings of dissonance … and pressure to do things a certain way' (p. 616). This pressure to do things in certain ways, located within the ideological parapets of Western institutions, poses unique challenges for Indigenous academics.

The experiences of Indigenous peoples entering academia and the efficacy of formal and informal mentoring has similarly been a site of interest. Burgess and Dyer (2009) provided a detailed outline of culturally specific considerations to be taken into account when establishing mentoring relationships with Indigenous peoples. Unfortunately, and perhaps this speaks to the age of their offering, their language tends to position Indigenous peoples not simply as marginalised but as deficient and different. The 'issues' faced by Indigenous peoples are positioned as challenges that stem from a difference inherent in Indigenous ways of being rather than a direct impact of colonisation through the operations of Western higher education institutions. This thinking has underpinned Indigenous inclusion strategies for decades. Indigenous support units have been established in many institutions across Australia. In a positive sense, they offer culturally safe spaces where future Indigenous leaders develop networks and friendships. They are also sites where mentoring relationships are encouraged. However, seen by some as distinct and separate enclaves, Nakata (2004) suggests they are also easily pointed to by institutions as the site of Indigenous problems, outside of the core faculties of the institution. Formal mentoring experiences, for Indigenous people, still carry the residue of hegemonic Western practices which either position Indigenous peoples as fundamentally ill-suited and in need of a chaperone or exclude them entirely. As Povey et al. (2022) highlight in their review of mentorship literature, formal mentoring programs in higher education may 'fail to support the growth of Indigenous cultural wealth in a system founded on Western epistemologies' (p. 11). A shift toward acknowledging the interface of Western and Indigenous knowledges in academia and genuine inclusion of Indigenous academics' perspectives in the planning and implementation of mentoring programs is needed.

Recent scholarship by Locke et al. (2021) looks at the logistics of mentoring possibilities as well as the desires of Indigenous Early Career Researchers. They highlight that there is a recognised scarcity of Indigenous senior academics at institutions across Australia and as such securing the engagement of an Indigenous mentor may prove difficult. This is backed up by *Universities Australia: Indigenous Strategy First Annual Report* (2019) into the state of Indigenous engagement in higher education, which highlights the continuing shortfall in Indigenous participation, especially in senior roles. As Indigenous Early Career Researchers look for mentoring opportunities it can be difficult to find a current Indigenous senior academic mentor who is not already overburdened with excessive workloads.

Despite this shortfall, my experience suggests senior Indigenous academics are still routinely sought after by Indigenous Early Career Researchers as the preferred providers of mentorship. This poses an urgent problem for academic institutions. How can we increase Indigenous leadership and representation in senior academic positions? One way is to grow our own. There are already a growing number of Indigenous scholars in Australia and around the world. In 2017 Trudgett et al. (2017) highlighted the immense contributions Indigenous peoples have made to the academy despite still being underrepresented A year later, Fredericks and White (2018) noted the considerable contribution of Indigenous women to the academy. The reflective scholarship that tracks the growth of Indigenous contributions to the academy often demonstrates the clear commitment to growing our own that Nakata (2006) pointed to in his commitment to community.

3 Formal or Informal Mentoring?

Institutions offer formal mentoring programs. This is a clear recognition of the value of building doctoral candidates' careers and easing the transition to Early Career Researcher status (Merga & Mason, 2021). However, for Indigenous peoples these mentoring programs still originate within a problematic institution that has a jaded past with Indigenous people and communities. In my experience, formal mentoring relationships arranged without input from Indigenous academics tend to be uncomfortable and provide very little benefit to either party. In one instance, related to me by a friend, the lack of foresight in proposing a mentorship opportunity was such that a senior Indigenous colleague was offered a formal mentorship arrangement where the mentor was a more junior non-Indigenous academic.

Informal mentoring is a recognised structure of mentoring relationships (Reis & Grady, 2020). Sometimes called alternative mentoring, it involves a shared set of 'beliefs that inform the boundaries of the relationship and promote equal sharing of ideas' (p. 32). Informal mentoring relationships are crucial to career building for Indigenous academics. The flexibility of structure allows the establishment of a partnership that acknowledges the problematics of Western academic institutions, privileges the perspectives of Indigenous scholars (both mentor and mentee), and encourages solutions to the question of career development and success at the site of what Nakata (2007) calls the 'cultural interface' of Western and Indigenous Knowledges.

My personal experiences of mentorship in the academy have been immensely positive. I have experienced informal mentorship in an environment which places high value on reciprocity and creating a collaborative atmosphere. One of the core philosophies of our team's work is to centre our commitment to Indigenous communities and future Indigenous scholars. Not only has this resulted in positive outcomes in my academic career, but it has provided me with the support to establish myself as an Indigenous academic strategizing institutional approaches to Indigenous higher education. In 2020, as part of the commitment of the Centre for Global Indigenous Futures to Indigenous Higher Degree Research candidates (HDR), I designed and delivered an inaugural Indigenous HDR Internship program. A paid, year-long program of workshops and informal collaborations which covers research, teaching, and community engagement aspects of academic careers, this Internship is aimed at demystifying higher education. It responds to the history of Indigenous exclusion in higher education and prepares junior academics for employment towards the end of their candidature.

My personal experience as a Higher Degree Research candidate, before establishing informal mentorship connections, was one where I was shielded from institutional operations. I was encouraged to publish just once and was offered very little teaching training despite a high sessional academic workload. I was invited to participate in undergraduate support programs based on my identification as an Indigenous person but given very little institutional support to carry out any meaningful community engagement activities. The desire that I felt to be more engaged and to learn about academic life during my doctoral candidature inspired my work towards building the Internship program. The Internship positions the academy as problematic for Indigenous people, rather than the other way around, and builds individual skill sets and knowledge of academia.

What I see in Indigenous academic spaces is community. There is a clear understanding, in many of these offices, faculties and departments, that Indigenous research has both had a troubled past and has an immensely promising future. Those with whom I surround myself see the role of collaboration, communication, and responsibility to other Indigenous peoples as core to any Indigenous academic's day-to-day work. This involves informal mentoring relationships, mutual navigation of the sometimes contradictory processes and procedures on campus, and operating in culturally meaningful and appropriate ways.

4 Conclusion

Mentoring is a valuable aspect of an Indigenous academic's professional development as much as it is for anyone. For Indigenous scholars working in higher education though, we acknowledge that the troubled history of relationships between Indigenous peoples and Western institutions still echoes through institutional policy and procedure. Walking the corridors of these institutions in the footsteps of the Indigenous academics that have only recently come before us, we are reminded that Indigenous knowledges and perspectives are still not always welcome across the board. It is my concern that the idea of formal mentoring in these Western institutions is too often seen as a response to an Indigenous need based on deficiency. Such assumptions are misguided, damaging, and downright demeaning. Grounding the need for mentorship in deficit thinking is not a fruitful position from which to establish a meaningful and successful career in any industry.

In building a career in academia one must remember that we, Indigenous scholars, chose to enter academia. We knew that the institutions we were walking into were overwhelmingly Western. Taking inspiration again from Nakata, I see this personal choice to remain a part of the institution as an opportunity for one more Indigenous scholar to engage with Western scientific thought, to understand the collisions between Western and Indigenous ways of knowing and being, and to forge ahead to produce new knowledge that draws on a much broader epistemological and ontological frame of reference found at the site of this collision. As Indigenous scholars continue mentoring the next generations in ways that are meaningful to us, we can continue toward exciting Indigenous academic futures.

References

Ambler, T., Harvey, M., & Cahir, J. (2016). University academics' experiences of learning through mentoring. *The Australian Educational Researcher, 43*(5), 609–627. https://doi.org/10.1007/s13384-016-0214-7

Burgess, J., & Dyer, S. (2009). Workplace mentoring for Indigenous Australians: A case study. *Equal Opportunities International, 28*(6), 465–485. https://doi.org/10.1108/02610150910980774

Fredericks, B., & White, N. (2018). Using bridges made by others as scaffolding and establishing footings for those that follow: Indigenous women in the Academy. *Australian Journal of Education, 62*(3), 243–255. https://doi.org/10.1177/0004944118810017

Krishna, L. K. R., Tan, L. H. E., Ong, Y. T., Tay, K. T., Hee, J. M., Chiam, M., Chia, E. W. Y., Sheri, K., Tan, X. H., & Teo, Y. H. (2020). Enhancing mentoring in palliative care: An evidence based mentoring framework. *Journal of Medical Education and Curricular Development, 7.*

Locke, M. L., Trudgett, M., & Page, S. (2021). Indigenous early career researchers: Creating pearls in the academy. *The Australian Educational Researcher.* https://doi.org/10.1007/s13384-021-00485-1

Merge, M. K., & Mason, S. (2021). Mentor and peer support for early career researchers sharing research with academia and beyond. *Heliyon, 7*(2), e06172. https://doi.org/10.1016/j.heliyon.2021.e06172

Nakata, M. (2004). Ongoing conversations about Aboriginal and Torres Strait Islander research agendas and direction. *Australian Journal of Indigenous Education, 33*(1), 1–6.

Nakata, M. (2006). Australian indigenous studies: A question of discipline. *The Australian Journal of Anthropology, 17*(3), 265–275. https://doi.org/10.1111/j.1835-9310.2006.tb00063.x

Nakata, M. (2007). The cultural interface. *The Australian Journal of Indigenous Education, 36*(S1), 7–14.

Povey, R., Trudgett, M., Page, S., Locke, M. L., & Harry, M. (2022). Raising an Indigenous academic community: A strength-based approach to Indigenous early career mentoring in higher education. *The Australian Educational Researcher*, 1–16.https://doi.org/10.1007/s13384-022-00542-3

Reis, T., & Grady, M. (2020). Moving mentorship to opportunity for women university presidents. *Faculty Publications in Educational Administration.* https://digitalcommons.unl.edu/cehsedadfacpub/124

Trudgett, M., Page, S., & Sullivan, C. (2017). Past, present and future: Acknowledging Indigenous achievement and aspiration in higher education. *Review of Higher Education.* https://opus.lib.uts.edu.au/handle/10453/121948

Universities Australia. (2019). *Indigenous Strategy First Annual Report*. Accessed June 3, 2022 from https://www.universitiesaustralia.edu.au/publication/indigenous-strategy-2022-25

Professor Tristan Kennedy is a Noongar Aboriginal man, and a member of the Kaurna community in South Australia and the South-West Aboriginal Land and Sea Council in Western Australia. After five years working in the Department of Indigenous Studies at Macquarie University, he was recently appointed Professor and Pro Vice-Chancellor (Indigenous) at Monash University. Tristan has contemporary research interests, attracting growing international interest and collaboration in areas such as identities in online social spaces, Indigenous studies and education, and digital communication technologies.

Open Access This chapter is licensed under the terms of the Creative Commons Attribution 4.0 International License (http://creativecommons.org/licenses/by/4.0/), which permits use, sharing, adaptation, distribution and reproduction in any medium or format, as long as you give appropriate credit to the original author(s) and the source, provide a link to the Creative Commons license and indicate if changes were made.

The images or other third party material in this chapter are included in the chapter's Creative Commons license, unless indicated otherwise in a credit line to the material. If material is not included in the chapter's Creative Commons license and your intended use is not permitted by statutory regulation or exceeds the permitted use, you will need to obtain permission directly from the copyright holder.

Paving the Way from Latchkey Kid to Big Sky Dreaming

Corrinne T. Sullivan

Yamma Dummarung

I am Wiradjuri. My family are from Trangie and Gin Gin Weir. My great grandfather seeking work on the railroads (a rare space where a black man could be employed and get paid) moved his family to Surry Hills, Sydney, this is where my beloved grandmother was born. I was raised during my younger years on D'harawal Country, later moving to Dharug Country where I continue to live and work.

1 Introduction

I grew up in a small rural town on D'harawal Country, the primary school could fit the entire student body on less than half a basketball court. The local high school was two towns over. I do not recall much conversation in my household around aspirations for educational attainment, rather, it was what we did due to the legislated mandate that kids go to school because they had to. My grandmother would often speak of the importance of being educated and the privilege of going to school. The rationale for schooling in my family was rarely an intellectual pursuit, alternatively, it was the gap before employment. Employment meant you entered the working class, an income that paid the bills was all that mattered. The family narrative was one of struggle, doing it tough, robbing Peter to pay Paul, and if you were lucky, making ends meet with a little bit left over which was stringently saved for a rainy day. Aspirations and flights of fantasy only occurred on occasions when talk turned to what you would do

---

C. T. Sullivan (✉)
Geography and Urban Studies, School of Social Sciences, Western Sydney University, Parramatta, NSW, Australia
e-mail: corrinne.sullivan@westernsydney.edu.au

if you won lotto—it seemed to my young self that the only path to success, economic or otherwise, was at the whim of seven balls.

By the time it came for me to go to high school we had moved to Dharug Country. I cannot say that I was a dedicated student, my job, as I saw it, fashioned from the perspectives of those around me, was to turn up and to stay out of trouble—I did not do my best, but I mostly turned up, and I mostly stayed out of trouble. I rarely did homework nor completed many assignments, no one at home checked my grades or read my report cards. I was placed in the higher classes for most subjects, I remain to this day really, really bad at math. Somehow without doing much of anything, I knew enough to get through. I completed year 10, then dropped out of high school a couple of weeks into year 11. I could not see the point in continuing school, I knew that I would not apply myself in the way I needed to finish well. In any case what was the point of staying in school? Whether I left having finished year 10 or year 12, the outcome to me was the same. I would finish school, and then I would get a job. Dropping out and earning money was highly appealing, I would have money to support myself and to help provide for my younger siblings. My mother did not care that I dropped out of school, though I was cautioned that I either had to go back to school or get a job. Three days after dropping out of school I got a job as a cashier at the local supermarket. I thought I was rich, and that I had made it.

2   I Am Restless

The thing with me is I get bored easily and become restless. It was not long into my cashier job that I wanted more. I was bored out of my mind and needed to do something else. I enrolled in vocational education to learn office skills. With some qualifications behind me, I was able to obtain work in administration roles, but often found myself becoming restless and wanting more. Reflecting on my work trajectory, I can identify the patterns of restlessness that sprang from the boredom that infected me once I had mastered whatever job I was doing with an impatience to move to something else. When moving to the next thing it was often accidental opportunities rather than purposeful aspirations, or perhaps it was some form of cosmic fate.

It was in 1999 that my life course shifted and led me to where I am today. I was 21 years old, a single parent to a nine-month-old baby, poor, and isolated, therefore, bored out of my brain and struggling to survive. I went to my local Aboriginal organisation and met with the employment manager to see what work was available—I wanted a job, any job, I did not care. On this fateful day someone else dropped by to catch up with the employment manager, he told me that he knew someone at Macquarie University that were looking to hire someone for a couple of weeks to do admin work. The following Monday I started. I had never stepped foot in a university until that day. To me, university was something of a dream, there was not much talk about university for me growing up. I am not even sure when I became aware that it was even a thing. The first person to get a degree in my family was my eldest cousin, perhaps this was the first time I heard of this being a thing. I never expected to go to university. I did not think anyone else thought I would either. I was wrong. Some years ago, my mother told me that one of my high school teachers had told her that I could go to university, that I had what it took. I felt incredulous that she never did anything about it, or at least spoke to me about it, though to be fair she would not have known what to do even if she had. She pressed that it was the teacher's job, I suspect the teacher thought it was the parent's job—there is much to unpack here around responsibility in education, but that is another chapter for another day. I digress.

Back to my first few weeks at Macquarie University. One task I was charged with was clearing the assignment boxes. I had to collect the assignments from the box, date/time stamp them, then disseminate to tutors for marking. I would often coincide this job with my lunch break so that I could read what students had written. I remember thinking, 'I could do that'. I found myself looking at university degrees and entry requirements. In early 2000 I enrolled in my first-degree program, with a one-year-old baby, and a full-time job. I had secured full-time work at Macquarie University off the back of those few weeks work—incidentally I was employed at Macquarie University for 20 years, in that time moving from professional roles to academic positions. I was fortunate in that I could attend classes around my work schedule, I would study during my lunch breaks, and after I put the baby to bed. It was tough but I loved it.

3 Becoming Academic

I eventually finished my Bachelor's Degree and was employed in a professional job in the library at Macquarie University. I was bored, and I wanted more. As fate would have it the Indigenous Student Support Officer role in the Indigenous Student Centre at Macquarie University was vacant. I desperately wanted that job. I felt that I had the right skills, experience and knowledge to be successful in the role. I emailed the then Director of the centre and asked for a chance. The cheek! To my delight she agreed. I loved that job and held it for several years. Eventually and in true form, I wanted more. I was considering undertaking an honours degree, but I did not know what I would study. By chance or perhaps fate, a box of dresses was delivered to the centre, they were interesting and reminded me of the kind of dresses that Aboriginal kids were dressed in on the missions and at institutions (Franklin, 2011). One of my colleagues directly challenged me, 'There's an honours project in that'. The very next day I had a meeting with a potential supervisor, soon after I applied to do an honours degree.

I completed my honours part-time, still working full-time, and a parent to two children. It was incredibly hard work, but I persevered with enormous support from my colleagues and supervisors. I completed my Honours Degree in 2011 and was awarded the University Medal for my efforts. I had been told that if I earned first class honours I would be able to then enrol straight into a PhD, and the potential to be seconded from my professional role as the Indigenous Student Support Officer to an Associate Lecturer (Level A Academic). From then to the completion of my PhD, I received several awards from within the University and from external bodies, both for Research, and Learning and Teaching. In one particular year across this time, I had been awarded a Learning and Teaching award, and a separate Research award—a colleague from within my discipline, it's Human Geography by the way, came up to me and said, 'Enjoy this, you will never have another year like it'. I note that in reading what was said to me that the words seem innocuous, perhaps even celebratory. They were not. It was the way and the tone in which they were delivered. You feel it, you know it's bad, just like the way you know whether an avocado is good or not—you feel it, you just know it! Sometimes you hope that maybe you were wrong about someone, not that I particularly cared for this person, but I still hoped I was wrong. Over several years up till now I have witnessed and been told several stories about this person's lack of support for, and what I think comes from an absolute disdain of Indigenous students and staff. Unfortunately, over the years I have encountered many people, students and staff, at every university in which I have worked or studied, who have been blatantly racist, openly condescending, and performing a plethora of microaggressions against Indigenous peoples. I suspect that every Indigenous student and staff member have both witnessed and have borne the brunt of these kinds of behaviours. These behaviours often leave me feeling that I must prove that I am just as good, I do this by giving twice as much, yet still regularly feel that I am only seen as mediocre at best. The struggle is real! But this chapter is not about them, it is about me, so…

Despite, or in spite of, the seemingly esoteric nature of universities and the iniquitous behaviour of some who haunt those spaces, I cannot help but feel that I am exactly where I should be. Although universities were never built for Indigenous peoples, I suspect that we were the last people that the architects of the archaic institution could ever imagine taking up space. Yet here we are, here I am. The genesis of Indigenous participation in universities was geared by the 1970's era of equity and access to higher education, thusly providing entry to those buildings and into the classrooms for the forerunners who paved the way forward for many of us to benefit from. It is our right to be here. I reject the ideology that university spaces are not for Indigenous people, although universities still suffer from their colonio-centric hangovers with their twisted and fraught systems and structures organised to work against Indigenous peoples, we must continue to maintain and hold that space. Even though for a spell those university spaces and their pale/stale architects tried to keep us out, those spaces, those buildings, rest on Indigenous land, that land has held, translated and transferred knowledge since the beginning. In turn that knowledge has been shared, learnt and taught by the people before us, our ancestors, and now (at least in part) by us. As Indigenous peoples we have always been educators and educated, simultaneously student and teacher.

4 Big Sky Dreaming

From my beginnings as an academic in 2012 to now in 2022, I have always wanted more, my restless nature has served me well. I worked my way from Associate Lecturer to Lecturer at Macquarie University. In 2018 I moved to Western Sydney University to take a position as Senior Lecturer, since that time I successfully applied for promotion to Associate Professor. I completed my PhD in 2020 (Sullivan, 2020) also in that year I was appointed to the position of Associate Dean (Indigenous Education) in the School of Social Sciences at Western Sydney University. In universities I found my place, I labour in service of my/our communities. I see the most important elements of the work I do is to create more space/s for Indigenous peoples, Indigenous Knowledges, Indigenous education. I aspire to do well. I was a latchkey kid, directionless, with no real dreams. However, in university I learnt to dream, to dream big. I have tracked my way through universities, through the academy, by imagining a different future for me, for my family, for my communities, for our collective communities. I am able to do so thanks to those that came before me, I am indebted to them for paving the way into the academy. It is now my obligation and my privilege to achieve this. There remains those that try to squash my dreams but I won't let them, I weaponise their underestimation of me against them—they rarely see me coming! My achievements to date have been built on a purposeful succession of small and large goals. Fate bought me into the university space, and its determination, ambition and discipline keeps me there. The university is my space and I aspire to command that space so that collectively we can maintain and control our sovereign right to it.

References

Franklin, C. (2011). *Moral Linen: Indigenous and non-Indigenous inmate experiences of dress in Parramatta Girls Home.* (Unpublished thesis), BA (Hons), Department of Environment and Geography, Macquarie University, Sydney.

Sullivan, C. T. (2020). *Indigenous Australian experiences of sex work: Stories of agency, autonomy and self-determination.* (Unpublished doctoral dissertation), Department of Geography and Planning, Macquarie University, Sydney.

Professor Corrinne Sullivan is an Aboriginal scholar from the Wiradjuri Nation in Central-West New South Wales. Her research interests are multi-disciplinary and focus broadly on experiences and effects of body and identity in relation to Aboriginal and Torres Strait Islander peoples. Corrinne's Honour's thesis entitled, 'Moral Linen: Indigenous and non-Indigenous experiences of dress in Parramatta Girls Home' was awarded the University Medal in Human Geography (2012). Her doctoral research explored the lived experiences of Aboriginal sex workers, Corrinne's thesis 'Indigenous Australian experiences of sex work: Stories of Agency, Autonomy and Self-Determination' was awarded the Vice-Chancellor's Commendation for Academic Excellence (2020). Corrinne's current work includes Indigenous and non-Indigenous experiences of sexuality and gender diversity through the perspectives of youth, older people, and sex workers.

Open Access This chapter is licensed under the terms of the Creative Commons Attribution 4.0 International License (http://creativecommons.org/licenses/by/4.0/), which permits use, sharing, adaptation, distribution and reproduction in any medium or format, as long as you give appropriate credit to the original author(s) and the source, provide a link to the Creative Commons license and indicate if changes were made.

The images or other third party material in this chapter are included in the chapter's Creative Commons license, unless indicated otherwise in a credit line to the material. If material is not included in the chapter's Creative Commons license and your intended use is not permitted by statutory regulation or exceeds the permitted use, you will need to obtain permission directly from the copyright holder.

Faith, Dreams and Lessons

Marcelle Townsend-Cross ⓘ

1 Introduction

I began my Early Career Researcher (ECR) journey on completion of my PhD at age of 56, after a 19-year career teaching Indigenous Studies in higher education. My commitment to teaching, learning and research in Indigenous Studies is motivated by my lived experience as a mixed-heritage First Nations member of the Stolen Generations and grounded in what Nakata (2004) describes as a 'definitive commitment to Indigenous people first and foremost, not to the intellectual or academic issues alone' (p. 2). It is a commitment to the pursuit of social justice for First Nations peoples across Australia who have never ceded their sovereignty and maintain their rights to their heritage, their cultural integrity and to self-determination. I acknowledge my Biripi/Worimi ancestors, Elders and family, Gadigal Custodians of the Country of my birthplace, and Awabakal Custodians of the Country I was privileged to learn and grow throughout my childhood and young adulthood. I acknowledge Widjabal/ Wyabal ancestors, Elders and communities on whose Country my family and I have been nurtured for the past 30 plus years and, to quote the dedication in my thesis, I acknowledge the First Nations 'women and men who have, through their wisdom and acumen since the imposition of colonisation, blazed the scholarly trail that I now humbly tread' (Townsend-Cross, 2018, p. v).

M. Townsend-Cross (✉)
University Centre for Rural Health, Faculty of Medicine and Health, University of Sydney, Goonellabah, NSW, Australia
e-mail: marcelle.townsendcross@sydney.edu.au

© The Author(s) 2025
M. Trudgett et al. (eds.), *Indigenous Early Career Researchers in Australian Universities*, SpringerBriefs in Education,
https://doi.org/10.1007/978-981-97-2823-7_14

2 My PhD Journey

In reflecting on my ECR journey, I am compelled to begin by sharing my experiences of pursuing postgraduate qualifications. This is an important part of my story toward pursuing a research career. Waiting until my 50s to undertake doctoral study was determined by a relatively late start to my career at age 37, and significantly, a lack of support and opportunity in the first 10 years of my career. While I embarked on my undergraduate degree at the not-so-old age of 23, the three beautiful babies that soon followed and the need to work to support them meant that my studies often had to take a back seat. It took nine years, but I got there in the end and graduated in 1996.

My academic career began in 1999 when, armed with only my undergraduate degree, I was lucky enough to win an associate lectureship through an Aboriginal employment strategy at a regional university in my hometown. I relished this role and thew myself into it, and after six years of dedicated teaching and administrative service, I began to seek support from the university to undertake postgraduate studies to progress my career. Despite the rhetoric of universities to prioritise support for First Nations postgraduate attainment, it took four years of self-advocacy, and in the end, the advocacy of the National Tertiary Education Union on my behalf, to succeed in getting enough support to undertake and graduate from a Masters Degree in 2009. My sights were now firmly set on doctoral studies, but it became evident that this would be impossible at my university as I had exhausted all avenues of support.

The following year I took up a position with another regional university within commuting distance from my hometown. The university offered a workload that afforded a 40 percent research component that I was able to dedicate to my doctoral studies on the condition that I completed my PhD by the end of a three-year probation period. Due to extended family-carer responsibilities and the passing of several close family members, I failed to complete my studies in the allocated timeframe and was offered a 12-month extension of my probation period. By this time, I was impatient to get on with my doctoral studies without interruption, because after all, I wasn't getting any younger. So, I took a leap of faith, resigned and began applying for scholarships. I succeeded in winning a decent scholarship that enabled me to continue to support my family whilst studying full-time. Three years later I submitted my thesis which was conferred in 2018.

3 My ECR Journey

At my graduation, I was offered a substantive position at the university where I had undertaken my doctoral studies. The role was perfect for my skill set and research interests and would have afforded me the training and research opportunities I needed to begin my ECR journey. The position required me to relocate from my regional hometown to Sydney, over 700 km away and unfortunately, my family responsibilities meant that this was impossible. I requested an opportunity to negotiate a mix of work-from-home and block attendance on campus, but my request was denied. Perhaps the outcome of my request would have been different had it been two years later in Covid-19 times, when working-from-home became not only common, but a requirement in many instances.

The first few years after graduating were spent working casually for several universities, the one in my hometown and an offshore university that operated in my local region. The casualisation of the workforce in Australian universities meant there were few substantive positions available across the state, let alone in regional areas. Without a substantive position at a university, I was unable to access ECR training programs because they were not offered to casual employees and, as a casual, it was difficult to find opportunities to undertake research. During this time, I came to regret resigning from my position at the university to take up full-time studies. If I had been more patient and stayed in the role, I might have had the opportunities I needed to begin my ECR journey.

Nevertheless, working as a casual at the university in my hometown, the university where I had begun my academic career, meant that I had established, long-term professional relationships with colleagues who offered informal support, advice and encouragement. I was also lucky enough to be a part of a supportive all-female teaching team who invited me to join them in undertaking a small research project focussing on our experiences as minoritised academics. We co-wrote two articles reporting on our research and were successful in publishing them in high-ranking peer reviewed journals. My ECR journey had finally begun! I remain very grateful to these women who, as mid-career researchers, supported and encouraged me and generously took the time to provide the advice I needed to continue to develop my research and writing skills.

Around the same time, after reading my published thesis, a long-term colleague invited me to contribute a chapter to an edited book alongside an impressive list of contributors. This opportunity enabled me to publish some of the key findings of my doctoral research and to further develop my writing skills. The book was published by Routledge two years later: the process of writing and submitting the chapter was just as valuable as being published. I learned so much from the critical and constructive feedback provided by the book's editors. Similarly, I learned a lot from the feedback from the peer reviewers of the journal articles co-authored with my colleagues. I came to realise that writing and submitting for publication is such an important part of the ECR journey, so I turned my sights to prioritising the editing of my thesis into journal articles to submit for publication. This remains a priority focus for me.

The opportunities to undertake small steps toward progressing my ECR career inspired me to dream bigger. I dreamt of creating my own opportunities to progress my research career. I reasoned that if my family responsibilities limited my opportunities to those accessible from my locale, then I needed to find a way to progress my career independent of the need to have a substantive position at a university. While my casual teaching roles enabled me to continue to practice in my preferred research context, the teaching and learning space, the roles were not necessarily focussed on the particular teaching and learning contexts that would enable me to pursue my research interests. This thinking-outside-the-box resulted in the idea to establish a consultancy business offering professional development training in the higher education sector. I promoted my consultancy through my established networks and landed my first consultancy in February 2020, just before the outbreak of the Covid-19 pandemic in Australia.

As the year progressed my casual teaching opportunities dwindled. Offshore students returned home as international borders closed and Australian universities, denied access to government wage subsidy measures, were in dire financial straits. The casual academic workforce bore the brunt of cost-cutting measures. About mid-year I was lucky enough to land a small research consultancy at my local university. The consultancy enabled me to continue my ECR journey and to earn enough to support my family for a while. Nonetheless, by early 2021, lockdown measures thwarted opportunities for progressing my consultancy and I was out of work and on unemployment benefits. Little did I know that just around the corner, lay an opportunity that I hadn't dreamt of and a lesson that I didn't know I needed.

The opportunity came about when I was sharing a cuppa with a neighbour. I was lamenting about having exhausted my (not insubstantial) networks for paid teaching and/or research opportunities in the local region. My neighbour asked me if I had applied for a position currently advertised by the University of Sydney based at the University Centre for Rural Health (UCRH) in my hometown. While the discipline of health was not one that I had worked in before, to my surprise the role perfectly fitted my skill set and would enable me to pursue my research interests. The lesson here was that I hadn't dreamt big enough or thought outside the box enough. Although I had been aware of the teaching and research work at the UCRH, I had never imagined that there could be a role there for me.

I applied for and won the position: a three-year, 0.8 contract at Level B with a balanced teaching and research workload. Working part-time enables me to fulfil my family responsibilities whilst progressing my ECR journey. At the time of writing, I am nine months into my contract and so far, it's the best job I've ever had. The workplace is dynamic, my skills are valued, research opportunities are plentiful, my colleagues are supportive and encouraging and I'm learning so much. All this, right in the centre of my hometown. I hadn't dared to dream so big, but I won't make that mistake again!

4 Conclusion

When I set out to write this reflective chapter about my ECR journey, I was encouraged to reflect on two particular questions. Would I do it again? Would I do it differently? The first question is easy. Yes! Unequivocally! The journey into research has been one of the most rewarding learning curves of my life. The second question is a little more complex. I certainly would have liked to begin my ECR journey sooner. Looking back, I had two opportunities to speed up and enhance the progress of my research career. The first opportunity was to stay in the job while I completed my doctoral research, the second opportunity was to take the position I was offered after graduation in Sydney. Both opportunities would have provided the institutional support I needed to launch my early research career in a timelier manner.

However, both options would have had significant impacts on my family. They would, in essence, have meant prioritising my career over my family responsibilities, something I have never been, and probably never will be, prepared to do. So, in the end, no, I wouldn't have done it any differently. In the end, I did it in the way that I had to do it, the way where I could move forward whilst being true to my family and true to my values. Who knows where I will be when my current contract comes to fruition in a few years. All I can do is dare to dream big, think outside the box, have faith in myself and keep moving forward.

References

Nakata, M. (2004). Indigenous Australian studies and higher education. In *The Wentworth Lectures* (pp. 1–20). Australian Institute of Aboriginal and Torres Strait Islander Studies.

Townsend-Cross, M. (2018). *Difficult knowledge and uncomfortable pedagogies:Student perceptions and experiences of teaching and learning in Critical Indigenous Australian Studies.* University of Technology Sydney. http://hdl.handle.net/10453/123274

Dr. Marcelle Townsend-Cross is a mixed heritage First Nations woman of Biripi, Worimi and Irish decent. Marcelle is an educator and researcher who currently teaches Aboriginal Studies at the University Centre for Rural Health for the University of Sydney. For over twenty years she has worked in higher education developing and delivering Indigenous Australian Studies subjects and degree courses at various universities. Marcelle holds a Ph.D. (2018) and a Master of Education (2009) from the University of Technology Sydney. Marcelle's Indigenous Australian heritage inspires her dual research focus on the history and contemporary manifestations and impacts of colonialism in Australia and on teaching and learning for social justice and social change.

Open Access This chapter is licensed under the terms of the Creative Commons Attribution 4.0 International License (http://creativecommons.org/licenses/by/4.0/), which permits use, sharing, adaptation, distribution and reproduction in any medium or format, as long as you give appropriate credit to the original author(s) and the source, provide a link to the Creative Commons license and indicate if changes were made.

The images or other third party material in this chapter are included in the chapter's Creative Commons license, unless indicated otherwise in a credit line to the material. If material is not included in the chapter's Creative Commons license and your intended use is not permitted by statutory regulation or exceeds the permitted use, you will need to obtain permission directly from the copyright holder.

Fishing Nets, River Banks and All the Things that Brought Me Here

Melinda Mann

When I was asked to write a piece for this book, a short reflective essay seemed to be the obvious writing style choice for me to capture my experiences and thoughts which I shared as a participant in the Indigenous Early Career Research (ECR) project. Reflection is something I do often not just for the purposes of retelling my story, one that I have recounted numerous times, but also as a way to self-assess against the ethics (for want of a better word) of my family, my Mob and my Old People. So, in telling my account of immersing in and emerging from a PhD program, I thought I would start with a story from my childhood in an attempt to make some sense of who I am.

Most of my childhood was spent at the beach, up rivers and down creeks in central Queensland and for a short time in western New South Wales. We fished … and we fished all the time. Sometimes we were sweltering under a midday sun or finding cover during a downpour. Whether it was summer or winter, fishing, cooking and eating fish has always been important to my family.

As we all know, fishing is a very popular pastime in Australia. But I think when Blackfullas go fishing it's a very different experience as a 'pastime'. I know I'm not alone in having learned as a young Blackfulla to be present in still moments, connecting with Country and talking with Ancestors when we are out fishing. I learned by observing my parents, aunties, uncles, and grandparents that getting away from town and spending time together fishing refreshed our spirits. These are some of the activities that keep us well. As a mother, these moments continue to be memorialised into my life as we pack cars in the still of the mornings, gather into convoys to head out 'for a fish'.

M. Mann (✉)
Central Queensland University, Rockhampton, Queensland, Australia
e-mail: m.m.mann@cqu.edu.au

© The Author(s) 2025
M. Trudgett et al. (eds.), *Indigenous Early Career Researchers in Australian Universities*, SpringerBriefs in Education,
https://doi.org/10.1007/978-981-97-2823-7_15

One of the lessons fishing taught me is the importance of waiting—waiting for the tides, for the fish to start or stop biting, for the sun to come up or go down, for the shade, for parents, for food, and sometimes with a lot of excitement waiting to catch fish with spears and nets. Sometimes we would put a net across an estuary and let it set until the tide changed in order to catch a large number of fish to fill the freezer (it's 'legal' to do this where I come from). As much as I loved being there to put the net in or take it out, I was only ever allowed once to swim the net across the creek. More often than not, my job was to hold the net bag. It wasn't an exciting job and I would sometimes struggle to hold the bag open under the weight of the wet hessian. I wanted to be the one to hook the bottom of the net around my leg, swim across the waterway and secure the end of the float line to an anchor point. It didn't matter how much I whinged and cried, it was always the bigger and stronger family members who were allowed to swim across the creek.

As the oldest daughter in my family and probably the least athletic amongst my cousins it always seemed like I would often be the one to do the uninspiring jobs like cleaning and looking after the younger ones. These lessons I learned from my parents, grandparents, aunties, uncles, and older cousins have helped me understand the way my life has been designed and shaped. I learned where I come from, who I come from, and who I am becoming. Importantly, I learned there are things that I can and cannot do, sometimes for my own safety and sometimes because it is simply not my role.

The concept of learning was something I had started to analyse even theorise as a child around the age of ten listening to my parents share stories of their childhood and adolescence as Aboriginal and South Sea Islander people. It was unsurprising to me that I would eventually end up with postgraduate qualifications in learning management and education. As a child, I would listen to my parents for hours and to anyone else of their generation or older talk about school, their teachers, and their experiences as learners. I was genuinely interested in understanding how all the Mob around me learned.

I would then spend days reflecting and admiring and sometimes agitating my young thoughts, linking stories, places, times and experiences. I had no knowledge of the government policies or legislation that impacted their schooling because they were Blackfullas but I was fully aware of their mistrust of White people and the prevalence of racism and trauma in their stories of schools. At this time, I was also constructing an understanding of how the classrooms I entered were never negotiated between Indigenous and non-Indigenous people to ensure my learning environment was free of racism. I remember becoming very aware in the last two years of primary school that I was being perceived by teachers and other students quite cautiously. My skin was dark, my grades were good and my mouth was cheeky. I was awarded numerous times for being conscientious and consistent and received top grades but I was regularly taunted by a teacher of another class in my year level for being poor and dark-skinned. My experiences of racism inside and outside of classrooms in the late 80s and early 90s were blatant. The racial slurs were relentless on my eleven-year-old body. And so began my imaginings of a future where I would focus on helping myself and other Blackfullas extract whatever we needed from Western education.

I do not believe that Mob ever need to be appreciative to a system of education that continues to indoctrinate Whiteness into sovereign Indigenous peoples regardless of the opportunities we have to access its various levels. Any appreciation I have is for my parents for teaching me how to unlearn the daily learnings of Whiteness while we sat at our dinner table each night in our Black home.

It was the mid-1990s when I commenced an undergraduate degree at Central Queensland University (Rockhampton campus). Before starting at CQU, I had never been in a place with so many people, and White people for that matter, in one location at one time. But, like so many other Blackfullas across Australian universities, I sought refuge in the Indigenous student unit. The friendships that were forged over assignments, listening to 90s Hip Hop and RnB music, laughter, food and other shenanigans have lasted a lifetime. I am so grateful for those friendships and the staff of the Indigenous student unit for their support and advocacy both of which were critical to me completing my Bachelor and Master Degrees and PhD.

Nine years after I graduated CQU with a Bachelor Degree in Business, I returned. I had three small children and I wanted to ensure I could provide for them on my own even though I was married at the time. When my youngest child was born, I was frustrated with being financially dependent on someone else. I enrolled in a bridging program usually undertaken by pre-undergraduate students. I was desperate to get a sense of whether I could think, write or speak at a postgraduate level. The Indigenous bridging program was tailored by Indigenous teaching staff to my needs and they built my academic confidence. The program has since been mainstreamed and the flexibility to negotiate participation is unfortunately no longer available.

In 2012, I graduated from the Masters of Learning Management course with Distinction and secured full time work at the same university just a week or two before my youngest child started formal schooling. In the final stages of the Masters course my Course Coordinator, a non-Indigenous woman named Dr Teresa Moore, propositioned me with the idea of doing a PhD and offering herself as primary supervisor. The proposal caught me by surprise. I was embarrassed. I had not even the slightest understanding of what a PhD involved nor what use it would be to me.

I knew very little about how programs and courses were designed and I was not connected with any Indigenous postgraduate students at my institution. Postgraduate program advice was difficult to access. It was through the National Indigenous Research and Knowledges Network (NIRAKN) that I began to fully appreciate the place, position and importance of postgraduate research for Indigenous people.

Dr Moore was critical to my PhD success. Her ability to guide and push me whilst simultaneously allowing me to learn, grapple, theorise and actuate my Indigenous ontology was a gift that reflects her passion for research. Although Indigenous PhD supervision was severely limited at my university, I persisted with Dr Moore from Masters to PhD. We had developed a trusting and respectful relationship and implemented mechanisms for accountability to the Darumbal Prescribed Body Corporate (PBC). Dr Moore insisted that approval for my research was sought from the PBC before the university ethics request was submitted and that two Darumbal peers who worked closely with the Native Title applicants on the PBC had input into every stage of the research. Both occurred and the impact on my research and myself as a researcher was immeasurable. The approval of the PBC is now a treasured communique for me. It spoke not of the importance of my research but of my importance as a Darumbal person. This bolstered my intentions to complete and deepened my commitment to prioritise cultural protocols and Indigenous methodologies.

My thesis was a collection of narratives, analysed for individual and collective understanding of young Aboriginal and Torres Strait Islander people who lived, at the time, on Darumbal Country. Country-centred enquiry of education and transition experiences helped elucidate ways young people were experiencing the concepts of belonging and becoming. Young Indigenous peoples' ability to navigate and articulate their roles in families, nation groups, the local Indigenous Community, and workplaces demonstrated astute uses of school environments and purposes for school not recognised by the education system. The resistance demonstrated by young Blackfullas in my research reiterated the rudimentary theorising I did as a child of school experiences of the adults around me.

My PhD program had commenced proper in late 2013 after experiencing long administration delays with my enrolment in 2012 and most of 2013. In 2016–2017 I took 12 months leave to focus on family issues and I submitted my thesis in December 2018 and graduated mid-2019. Throughout my PhD program, I worked within the university as a Professional (non-academic) staff member in management roles before becoming the Deputy Director of Student Life and Wellbeing. In this role, I had oversight of Indigenous and international student support, student counselling, careers service, schools outreach programs, scholarship administration, and accessibility service. I did short acting stints as Director of Student Experience (this role included the large student admissions centre) and Pro Vice-Chancellor Indigenous Strategy and chaired various committees and working groups across institutions. I was a single mother of two high school and one primary school aged children. Somehow the only sports training session we ever missed was the one my son skipped to attend my PhD graduation.

When I left the higher education sector almost twelve months after graduating with a PhD, I did so to grow myself intellectually and culturally within my community. I knew if I continued to pursue a career in the academy whether professional or academic, I would never find the time to learn in community directly from Darumbal Elders as they work constantly on building our Nation. In stepping away from the Academy I was refusing, as opposed to sacrificing, the opportunity to build my academic reputation.

It bothered me that I could be deemed an 'expert' on my PhD subject matter (i.e., learning on Darumbal Country) when the experts were all around me—my Elders. Imposter syndrome was not something I have struggled with. I live on my land and I know who I am. Rather, leaving the sector was because I have always known where to look for the signs that have designed my life. In order for me to go forward I need to go back—back to my Elders and to be a 'student' of theirs. My early career research period is devoted to my Mob's work outside of the academy and I imagine nation-building will be the most important work I can set my heart to. I maintain my link with the academy but it is by no means a substantial part of my work. In time

I will return but whether I do or not, belonging in or to the academy is not a high priority for me.

I am interested in exercising sovereignty and self-determination in the work I now do in my community as well as how I make decisions over this period of my career. I want to be loyal to the convictions I held as a Black youth and not to the aspirations Western education has for Indigenous students. It is in knowing how, where and by whom I was raised that I understand the value of education and research. As my dad, Rob Mann (senior), constantly reminds my siblings and I and our children 'Country [in all of its meaning] is the greatest teacher'.

My Indigenous early career research track is a new phase of my life where I learn and create learning more consistent with who I am as an Aboriginal woman than ever before. I have come to appreciate that while my writing is not being published in academic journals, it is being used in biographical and representational texts in various types of literary collections, on signs and didactics, in places and spaces that benefit Blackfullas by pushing against colonial narratives often prolific in regional and rural parts of this country.

That the title of 'Dr' by PhD is of little value outside of the academy sits very easily with me. I am annoyed when the title elicits a positive change in someone's behaviour toward me. I would much prefer to affect change and win arguments without it in all honesty than to be patronised by the reminder of the status it equates. This is not to say that I regret doing a PhD but rather that the process was far more important than obtaining a title. In having said that, I am moved by the pride in Mob's voices when they strategically use the title with my name to push against those ever-present colonial barriers. It gives me great joy to see the title that comes with my level of educational achievement be used by Mob as a weapon against the oppressors that granted it to me.

It is an honour to intentionally choose to be a community-based Early Career Researcher, living on Darumbal Country, investing my focus in Darumbal Nation building, working strategically with Darumbal peers to fulfill the aspirations of Darumbal Elders—doing all of this to be a good Darumbal Ancestor. This is sovereign work and there is nothing more of a priority for me then (re)building solid nations and claiming our place on our land and sea Country. I appreciate that battles in the academy still exist and are incredibly important. However, as an Indigenous ECR I want to emulate the professors and philosophers of Darumbal Country whose bloodlines I carry and whose knowledges I protect and privilege, knowing that sadly one day and likely all too soon I will be required to step into their roles. In the meantime, I am more than content to wait and to hold a metaphorical fishing net bag for my Elders, drawing from the lessons I learned on muddy river banks all those years ago. These are all the things that have brought me here.

Dr. Melinda Mann is a Darumbal and South Sea Islander woman, who lives and works on her homelands in Rockhampton, Queensland. She has over 25 years of experience in education and training. Melinda's scholarship draws from her professional experiences in school, tertiary and community education sectors; her lived experiences in regional and rural towns; and her commitment to nation building to assert First Nations sovereignty. She is a member of various advisory groups including a ministerial appointment to the Queensland Aboriginal and Torres Strait Islander Education and Training Committee.

Open Access This chapter is licensed under the terms of the Creative Commons Attribution 4.0 International License (http://creativecommons.org/licenses/by/4.0/), which permits use, sharing, adaptation, distribution and reproduction in any medium or format, as long as you give appropriate credit to the original author(s) and the source, provide a link to the Creative Commons license and indicate if changes were made.

The images or other third party material in this chapter are included in the chapter's Creative Commons license, unless indicated otherwise in a credit line to the material. If material is not included in the chapter's Creative Commons license and your intended use is not permitted by statutory regulation or exceeds the permitted use, you will need to obtain permission directly from the copyright holder.

Future Directions

Future Directions: Where the End is Actually the Beginning

Michelle Locke

Dear reader,

I thank you for taking the time to hear the voices of Indigenous Early Career Researchers (ECRs). Although, if you have come straight to this final chapter to decide if this book holds interest or relevance to you, I am here to say that this is not actually the end, it is only the beginning. If you are a non-Indigenous reader and are serious and genuinely committed to supporting the development of Indigenous ECRs with a view to raising the profile of Indigenous narratives and knowledges throughout educational institutions, then this book is a prerequisite to your actions. In order to challenge and change the status quo it is paramount to firstly listen and genuinely consider Indigenous voices to develop global academies that value and embrace diverse worldviews and epistemologies. If you are an Indigenous ECR, then you will likely find or have found kindred spirits who have had at least some of the same experiences as you have had. I hope you have found strength and purpose in the paths your colleagues have forged.

In this edited book 14 Indigenous ECRs genuinely and generously shared their knowledges, perspectives and personal experiences as scholars in the Australian higher education sector. Its publication signals the completion of a three-year longitudinal study funded by the Australian Research Council. The project titled *Developing Indigenous Early Career Researchers* sought to better understand the convoluted and creative career trajectories of Indigenous ECRs, as well as identifying some barriers and enablers that hinder and help Indigenous ECRs to building sound research trajectories, and careers in institutions across Australia. For this study, Indigenous ECRs were interviewed once each year for three years from 2020 to 2022, to facilitate the exploration of *'evolving and complex processes'* (Murray et al., 2009) associated with Indigenous academic career progression.

M. Locke (✉)
Western Sydney University, Kingswood, NSW, Australia
e-mail: m.locke@westernsydney.edu.au

Interestingly, the launch of this project coincided with the arrival of Covid-19 on Australian shores, which required a swift change of plan from in-person interviews to the use of zoom software. This has arguably become both the saviour and bane of professional and social interactions worldwide. With the use of zoom in 2020, 30 Indigenous ECRs from 21 different institutions across Australia were interviewed. Due to personal health issues that were surprisingly unrelated to Covid-19, the number of Indigenous ECRs participating in the project dropped to 28 in 2021 and stayed at that same number in 2022. Nevertheless, a total of 86 interviews were conducted over a period of three years. As a result, the research team drew on shared narratives and experiences that provided extensive insights into Indigenous ECR experiences and perspectives. These insights have been made available in national and international scholarly journals, at education conferences, and of course in the chapters of this book which are authored by the Indigenous ECRs.

As an Indigenous ECR, and the postdoctoral researcher on this project I wish to acknowledge the many and varied opportunities the *Developing Indigenous Early Career Researchers* project has provided me. Firstly, the opportunity to work with Senior Indigenous researchers and a non-Indigenous ECR colleague, all who were more than generous with their time in guiding and supporting me to navigate the institution in ways that have benefitted my developing career. Secondly, this project enabled me to build on my skills as a researcher and to grow my publication record, which is of course an important currency of a successful academic career. Thirdly and most significantly, I had the opportunity to meet and yarn with Indigenous ECRs across the country. Although Covid-19 severely restricted my ability to meet in person with many of these inspiring and generous people, their sharing of knowledges and stories strengthened my journey and resolve as an Indigenous ECR.

This sharing of wisdom borne of experience is why this book is a valuable resource for current and future Indigenous ECRs as well as all peoples engaged in the higher education sector. It is appropriate for Indigenous students to find strength and motivation in the achievements and aspirations of Indigenous ECRs who strive to create spaces in universities that provide culturally relevant and rewarding career opportunities and pathways. It is also paramount that non-Indigenous colleagues, mentors, supervisors, and university executives understand the challenges faced by Indigenous ECRs. With a deeper level of understanding non-Indigenous staff can work more respectfully with Indigenous peoples in providing genuinely accessible career pathways that more effectively employ Indigenous knowledeges and epistemologies in higher education institutions across Australia. Indigenous communities and the nation can only benefit from the fresh perspectives and research that these ECRs will undertake during their careers.

While it is crucial to understand the challenges faced by Indigenous ECRs in establishing sound research careers it is equally important to note the achievement of attaining a doctoral qualification and the continued efforts of centering Indigenous knowledges and perspectives in institutions that typically 'apply greater pressure on their early career academics to perform, conform and maintain status quo' (Povey et al., 2022a, 2022b). This book is a testament to all Indigenous ECRs studying, researching, and teaching in institutions across Australia.

1 Indigenous Connections and Responsibilities

While each chapter elucidates the diversity of Indigenous ECRs, it is also essential to note the attributes that unite Indigenous scholars and set us apart from non-Indigenous scholars.

In contrast to non-Indigenous scholars, success for Indigenous ECRs is not solely measured on attaining individual academic achievements or awards. In fact, from an Indigenous epistemological standpoint, relationality, responsibility and accountability to Country and kin are paramount (Martin, 2008). Thus, the conditions of success for an Indigenous scholar are complex and oftentimes conflicting. Like non-Indigenous scholars, Indigenous scholars are accountable to the rules and requirements of the academy. However, we are also and firstly accountable to Indigenous worldviews and the protocols of the Countries and communities to which we are related and connected. Research efforts and aspirations to improve outcomes for Indigenous peoples are often underestimated, under-valued or disregarded by non-Indigenous scholars, schools and/or institutions. This reflects the ongoing colonial project, in which Indigenous knowledges, languages, cultures and identities continue to be misrepresented, underestimated, and oftentimes misappropriated by and within institutions founded on and dominated by Western worldviews and values (Atkinson et al., 2010; Bodkin-Andrews & Carlson, 2016; Moreton-Robinson, 2015). This conflict is greatly exacerbated when institutions promote inclusion and equity on the one hand but also dictate restrictive roles and responsibilities of Indigenous ECRs and scholars where:

> Indigenous scholars are often treated as lesser as if their research offers little benefit to mainstream society and is therefore best placed within areas run by Indigenous people for Indigenous audiences, or in areas that provide a general education for non-Indigenous peoples. (Fredericks et al., 2023, p. 38)

In order to gain recognition as academic scholars and as culturally appropriate representatives of our communities Indigenous ECRs must successfully engage and meet the expectations of both Western and Indigenous systems of knowledge. (Locke et al., 2022a; Povey et al., 2022a, 2022b; Thunig & Jones, 2020). Consequently, each Indigenous ECRs' contribution to this book continually navigates and negotiates with the academy's Western-based systems of education to represent and raise the voices of Indigenous peoples and their communities in culturally respectful, appropriate and relevant ways. The achievements of these Indigenous ECRs, provides unequivocal evidence of Indigenous strength, wisdom and tenacity, which are characteristics that are arguably held in high regard by academics across the higher education sector.

Disappointingly, both Australian and international research authored by Indigenous and scholars stress the ongoing prevalence of both covert and overt racist attitudes, perspectives and assumptions about the roles, responsibilities and capacity of Indigenous academics (Baice et al., 2021; Bodkin-Andrews et al., 2021; Fredericks et al., 2023; Kidman, 2020; Locke et al., 2022a; Povey et al., 2022a, 2022b; Thunig & Jones, 2020). In order to develop sound research trajectories and be recognised as successful scholars, Indigenous ECRs must respectfully represent and engage two differing knowledge systems. However, in doing so, many also face racist views, biases and behaviours (Locke et al., 2022a; Povey et al., 2022a, 2022b). From this perspective, in order to meet cultural obligations and disrupt negative stereotypes, Indigenous scholars are often required to be more, deliver more and to do more than non-Indigenous scholars. This is the result of institutional environments that are often unsafe and toxic to Indigenous cultural identities and connections (Fredericks, 2011; Locke et al., 2022a; Thunig & Jones, 2020).

Povey, Trudgett, Page and Locke (2022a, 2022b) note that, 'in a stratified workplace, [Indigenous] ECRs are constrained by White walls and a 'calm violence' in a sector where the White benchmark continues to thrive, albeit hidden in plain view (p. 14)'. I ask that all readers stop and seriously consider this perspective. Reflect back on the barriers and hurdles identified and discussed by each Indigenous author. It is fair to say that some of these burdens may not appear to be that different to those faced by non-Indigenous ECRs such as building recognition for research via publication. However, in reading and deeply listening to these voices you will note that the academy is a colonised space (Kidman, 2020; Moreton-Robinson, 2015; Smith et al., 2021) and as such it is a contested space in which Indigenous peoples are often marginalised (Nakata, 2007). Yet, as the stories of the Indigenous ECRs in this book attest, they also find ways to resist, insist and flourish, forging more diverse pathways for the next generation of Indigenous scholars.

In truth, to create institutions in which social justice and equitable outcomes are realised all peoples must be involved. Commitment is required from students to senior executives to establish and maintain systemic approaches that provide appropriate opportunities for the development of Indigenous ECRs and the inclusion of Indigenous knowledges that align with Indigenous Ways of Knowing (Locke et al., 2022b).

2 How to Walk and Work with Indigenous Early Career Researchers

This book provides a window into the lives of Indigenous ECRs, who are already active changemakers across the higher education sector. Indigenous ECRs have and continue to navigate the academy with the strength, tenacity and agency required to not only identify barriers but to challenge and dismantle them. While each chapter shares differing personal perspectives and experiences, we share a common determination in honouring Indigenous peoples who have walked before us while at the same time building clear and lasting pathways for others to walk with and after us.

It is likely, that you would have engaged differently with each author and the perspectives they shared. It is also probable that there was at least one author that resonated more strongly with your own understanding and/or experience. Perhaps there was a chapter or two that didn't seem as relevant or important to your personal or professional life. However, this book was not designed to be read once and then put on a shelf and forgotten. It is highly likely that different chapters will resonate with you at different points in your own journey.

This book is a gift to Indigenous and non-Indigenous people, whether you are a scholar, educator, student, parent or any other person interested in the perspectives, experiences and knowledges of Indigenous peoples. This book openly shares Indigenous ECR narratives and experiences and requires you to think about the role you play in raising or silencing the voices of Indigenous peoples. For our non-Indigenous readers this book is designed as a companion to support your journey in understanding the value and validity of Indigenous peoples and knowledges to all peoples. When you choose to read and deeply consider the information shared in each chapter some of your own perspectives and beliefs may be strengthened and others are likely to be challenged. However, in genuinely contemplating these different points of view you will be provided with an invaluable opportunity to move beyond the overarching discourses that endorse the deficit positioning of Indigenous peoples. Each chapter of this book invited you into to a space in which you were urged to consider education, identity, and purpose from the perspective of those who have for too long been undervalued and/or silenced in Western-based institutions of research, teaching and learning.

If you yourself are an educator or scholar this journey, your journey will of course be influenced by your current position and role with or within educational institutions. You may be an Indigenous student or scholar in which case the authors in this book have offered strength, guidance and connection through their shared narratives and knowledeges. Alternatively, you may be a non-Indigenous student or scholar seeking a deeper understanding and perhaps an insight into the ways in which to work with and learn from Indigenous peoples, families and/or communities. Whichever perspective or position it is probable that different chapters will provide differing levels of sense and meaning at different stages in your learning journey.

3 If You Are an Indigenous Student, Scholar, Teacher, Elder or Community Member

The intention for this book was to not only raise the voices of Indigenous ECRs but to recognise, honour and celebrate all Indigenous Ancestors and peoples on whose shoulders we stand. Each author speaks to those that have cared, supported, guided, strengthened, and sometimes even 'growled' them to where they are today. In turn, Indigenous ECRs also recognised, promoted and championed the development and maintenance of pathways and opportunities for current and future Indigenous students, educators and academics in educational institutions across Australia.

It is hoped that this book offers a source of inspiration to all Indigenous peoples in highlighting the abilities and success of Indigenous ECRs across the higher education sector, however these narratives aspire to offer more than hope. These narratives engaged in truth telling about the challenges and stresses of Western-based institutions, such as Dr Skye Akbar who highlighted the pressure of being the sole Indigenous academic in a school where the demand for Indigenous knowledges and perspectives were high. Likewise, Associate Professor Katrina Thorpe provided specific advice to Indigenous ECRs on the topics of institutional expectations, avoiding distractions and seeking support to fully understand research funding requirements, while Dr BJ Newton shared eight rules for surviving academia. It is expected that Indigenous students, scholars, teachers, Elders and/or community members will have seen some aspect of themselves in the telling of these stories and that this connection will encourage you to understand the roles you have and can continue to play in building and raising Indigenous voices in the higher education sector across Australia.

For Indigenous students, teachers and academics, the purpose of this book was to acknowledge the challenges and burdens that can be faced by Indigenous peoples in educational institutions but more importantly to share a variety of responses and strategies that Indigenous ECRs have engaged to successfully navigate the system, whilst retaining their relationships and responsibilities to their Countries and communities. Both Professor Scott Avery and Dr Anthony McKnight specifically spoke to the wisdom of their Elders and of the strength and validity of cultural knowledges in an academic arena. For you this book has offered both guidance and support towards your journey in academia. Perhaps it will go as far as to strengthen your motivation and resolve to collaborate in a joint project in growing global academies that value and seek diversity through genuine respect, recognition and engagement of Indigenous peoples and knowledges.

4 If You Are a Non-Indigenous Educator

In order to build trust and walk with Indigenous scholars it is also necessary to seek out Indigenous voices in all the forms in which they are shared, including through song, poetry, art, dance, media, academic writing and conference presentations. It is up to you to engage in some deep listening and thinking. That is, rather than gathering these Indigenous knowledges and perspectives to add to your own resources, engage as a matter of critical self-reflection. Proud and Morgan (2021) highlight three key steps in critical self-reflection that they encourage teachers to engage in. The first step in this process is to *know your own cultural identity* (p. 40). This they note is a useful insight from the practices of Indigenous peoples. Specifically, Proud and Morgan (2021) note that it is essential, for teachers to have a strong understanding of one's own cultural identity prior to the effort of learning about a cultural identity that is different to their own. Secondly, Proud and Morgan (2021) encourage teachers to identify and understand social, cultural and historical influences that shape the way in which teachers view and interpret the world. Relatedly, in this book, Professor Corrinne Sullivan noted their repetitive experience of the underestimation of their skills and abilities in the academy and strongly advocated for the recognition of Indigenous agency. Finally, Proud and Morgan (2021) encourage educators to look for and acknowledge positive attributes of Indigenous peoples. They state that, 'due to deficit discourses that continue to shape the stereotypical perceptions of Indigenous peoples within Australia, teachers need to critically reflect upon their own stereotypes and biases' (p. 45). Critical self-reflection is a useful approach in opening yourself to perspectives and approaches that can both challenge and extend not only your own learning but also influence those you interact and collaborate with.

5 If You Are a Non-Indigenous Scholar or Educator

It is imperative that positive change for Indigenous peoples is not engaged from the position of benevolent benefactors. Research (Fredericks et al., 2023; Moodie, 2018; Povey et al., 2022a, 2022b; Rigney, 2001) has evidenced the fact that genuine and successful change requires guidance if not leadership from Indigenous peoples. Everyone can take an active role by firstly sourcing the works of Indigenous ECR authors in this book that both resonate and challenged you to think more critically and deeply. Read, share and cite these publications. As an academic you will know that recognition through citations helps to build a researcher's career trajectory, and, in this case, citing publications authored by Indigenous ECRs strengthens Indigenous voices and assists in centering Indigenous knowledges and perspectives in institutions dominated by Western epistemologies and worldviews. Moreover, when you seek out and read additional works of the Indigenous ECRs in this book you will be exposed to the knowledges, works and experiences of Indigenous and scholars that have inspired supported or are currently working with the Indigenous ECR.

Certainly, the voices of Indigenous ECRs in this book and in related research (Fredericks, 2011; Locke et al., 2022a; Thunig & Jones, 2020) identify issues that arise when Indigenous ECRs are positioned in token roles that only serve to meet expectations or requirements for Indigenous representation but are of no benefit to Indigenous ECRs career development or trajectory. As a non-Indigenous scholar or educator, it is your role to work with your Indigenous colleagues in a manner that supports and develops their career, but also creates opportunities and pathways to grow the number of Indigenous scholars within your school and institution. It is possible that you may have 'insider' knowledge to programs or opportunities that could further support the development and growth of an Indigenous ECR's academic trajectory and/or research profile. Which is not to say that it is your role or duty to dictate the direction or purpose of an Indigenous ECRs developing career, rather to develop respectful and meaningful relationships with Indigenous ECRs in order to gain a deeper understanding and appreciation of the agency, strengths, cultural connections, knowledges and aspirations they bring to the academy. Building relationships and connections fosters the opportunity to walk with these Indigenous scholars to address educational disparities. Using these strength-based approaches can challenge entrenched beliefs that Indigenous voice is somehow worth less to non-Indigenous people (Fredericks et al., 2023) and in doing so enable systemic changes that centre Indigenous Ways of Knowing.

6 For Institutions and University Executives

The underrepresentation of Indigenous scholars across the higher education sector (Coates et al., 2020; Fredericks et al., 2023; Uink et al., 2021) creates a significant burden on Indigenous ECRs. In their chapters, Dr Marcelle Townsend-Cross, Dr Robyn Ober and Dr Tristan Kennedy identified the need for Indigenous ECRs to find like-minded collaborators and Indigenous mentors to better understand and navigate the academy in order to develop sound career trajectories. It is not enough to employ one or two Indigenous scholars in a school or institution and expect policies of diversity and equity to be fully realised. In reading this book you would note that Indigenous ways of knowing prescribe intergenerational collaborative learning through the sharing of knowledges and resources that understand and respect cultural protocols recognising all aspects of Indigenous identity and belonging to Country (Burgess et al., 2022; Martin, 2008). Therefore, Indigenous ECRs and scholars should not be expected work in isolation. However, to grow the number of Indigenous scholars requires a concerted effort and commitment from institutions at an executive level. It is critical that policies of diversity and equity are active documents in which genuine actions, such as funding opportunities and programs that assist in providing access to culturally relevant mentors and supervisors for the development of Indigenous ECRs are actually implemented and maintained. Research supports the point that the availability of Senior Indigenous academics to act as mentors can affect positive results in the engagement and advancement of Indigenous ECRs (Fredericks et al., 2023; Povey et al., 2022a, 2022b; Uink et al., 2021).

Similarly, institutions must make all staff accountable to creating safe spaces in which stereotyping and racism are identified and perpetrators held to account. Without accountability, commitment to the inclusion of Indigenous peoples and knowledges becomes nothing more than lip service, which has been reported in recent literature as a reality of Indigenous experiences within the academy (Locke et al., 2022a; Povey et al., 2022a, 2022b; Thunig & Jones, 2020).

Many of the Indigenous ECRs participating in the '*Developing Indigenous Early Career Researchers*' project commented that it is at the executive level of institutions where the greatest power to affect positive change exists. Building an effective pipeline of Indigenous ECRs is one way to ensure the potential for greater Indigenous leadership across all areas of universities. This perspective is recognised and advocated by Universities Australia in their *Indigenous Strategy 2022–25*.

> It is vital that Vice-Chancellors and their senior management groups actively champion the Indigenous Strategy in their institution, in whole of sector governance bodies and other forums. Indigenous views should be represented at top level university forums such as meetings of the Council and senior executive. (p. 38)

This sets the scene for what can be achieved in global academies who genuinely accept responsibility to the creation of socially just institutions of education, in which diverse knowledges and worldviews are not only recognised but are valued, engaged and honoured.

7 For All Readers. What Kind of Ancestor Do You Want to Be?

To finish, I pose this final question to you the reader. If you are fortunate enough to live a long life and perhaps become a parent, grand parent or grand Aunt or Uncle, how would you like to be remembered by the generations that follow? In this book both Dr Vincent Backhaus, Dr Tracy Woodroffe and Dr Melinda Mann specifically noted the significant level of responsibility they feel in their roles as Indigenous ECRs to their Indigenous families and communities. If you had a choice, what legacy would you choose to leave those that will follow in your footsteps? Will you be remembered for the achievements that shaped and supported your own life and perhaps those immediate to you or do you hope to inspire future generations to question the status quo by engaging, participating and celebrating the diversity of Indigenous peoples, landscapes and the oldest living culture in the world?

From an Indigenous worldview, knowledge and learning is a shared experience across generations and through relationships, responsibility and reciprocity with all entities. Indigenous relationality prescribes that all peoples, plants, animals, landscapes, waterways, seas and skies are connected. From this position, no one is more important or knowledgeable than another, nevertheless everyone is responsible for and accountable to family, community, Country and all entities. Indigenous Ways of knowing, being and doing establish protocols in which Indigenous Ancestors and Elders are afforded much respect due to the wisdom, knowledges and stories of Country they hold. However, all peoples are known to have valuable knowledge and experiences to share. As stated by Bishop (2022), 'Our Old People have much to share, but also acknowledge they have much to learn from the young ones' (p. 141).

So, I return to my question, will you be remembered for the achievements that shaped and supported your own life or do you hope to inspire future generations to question the status quo. If your answer is the latter then I challenge you to start now. Take some time to travel back through this book and identify a goal or aspiration that speaks to you regarding Indigenous peoples and specifically to engaging, valuing and protecting the knowledges and perspectives that are unique to this country known now as Australia.

References

Atkinson, R., Taylor, E., & Walter, M. (2010). Burying indigeneity: The spatial construction of reality and Aboriginal Australia. *Social & Legal Studies, 19*(3), 311–330. https://doi.org/10.1177/0964663909345449

Baice, T., Lealaiauloto, B., Meiklejohn-Whiu, S., Fonua, S. M., Allen, J. M., Matapo, J., Iosefo, F., & Fa'avae, D. (2021). Responding to the call: Talanoa, va-vā, early career network and enabling academic pathways at a university in New Zealand. *Higher Education Research and Development, 40*(1), 75–89. https://doi.org/10.1080/07294360.2020.1852187

Bishop, M. (2022). Indigenous education sovereignty: Another way of 'doing' education. *Critical Studies in Education, 63*(1), 131–146. https://doi.org/10.1080/17508487.2020.1848895

Bodkin-Andrews, G., & Carlson, B. (2016). The legacy of racism and Indigenous Australian identity within education. *Race, Ethnicity and Education, 19*(4), 784–807. https://doi.org/10.1080/136 13324.2014.969224

Bodkin-Andrews, G., Foster, S., Bodkin, F., Foster, J., Andrews, G., Adams, K., & Evans, R. (2021). Resisting the racist silence. When racism and education collide. In M. Shay & R. Oliver (Eds.), *Indigenous education in Australia. Learning and teaching for deadly futures* (pp. 21–37). Routledge.

Burgess, C., Thorpe, K., Egan, S., & Harwood, V. (2022). Learning from country to conceptualise what an Aboriginal curriculum narrative might look like in education. *Curriculum Perspectives, 42*(2), 157–169. https://doi.org/10.1007/s41297-022-00164w

Coates, S., Trudgett, M., & Page, S. (2020). Indigenous higher education sector: The evolution of recognised Indigenous Leaders within Australian Universities. *Australian Journal of Indigenous Education*, 1–7. https://doi.org/10.1017/jie.2019.30

Fredericks, B. (2011). Universities are not the safe place we would like to think they are, but they are getting safer': Indigenous women academics in higher education. *Journal of Australian Indigenous Issues, 14*(1), 41–53. https://eprints.qut.edu.au/38492/

Fredericks, B., Bunda, T., & Bradfield, A. (2023). Indigenous women in Academia: Reflections on leadership. In A. Samad, E. Ahmed, & N. Arora (Eds.), *Global leadership perspectives on industry, society, and government in an era of uncertainty* (pp. 36–54). IGI Global. https://doi.org/10.4018/978-1-6684-8257-5.ch003

Kidman, J. (2020). Whither decolonisation? Indigenous scholars and the problem of inclusion in the neoliberal university. *Journal of Sociology, 56*(2), 247–262. https://doi.org/10.1177/144078 3319835958

Locke, M. L., Trudgett, M., & Page, S. (2022a). Australian Indigenous early career researchers: Unicorns, cash cows and performing monkeys. *Race, Ethnicity and Education*, 1–17. https://doi.org/10.1080/13613324.2022.2114445

Locke, M. L., Trudgett, M., & Page, S. (2022b). Building and strengthening Indigenous early career researcher trajectories. *Higher Education Research and Development*. https://doi.org/10.1080/07294360.2022.2048637

Martin, K. (2008). *Please knock before you enter: Aboriginal regulation of outsiders and the implications for researchers*. Post Pressed.

Moodie, N. (2018). Decolonising race theory: Place, survivance and sovereignty. In G. Vass, J. Maxwell, S. Rudolph, & K. N. Gulson (Eds.), *The relationality of race in education research. Local/global issues in education* (1 ed., pp. 33–46). Routledge. https://doi.org/10.4324/978131 5144146-3

Moreton-Robinson, A. (2015). *The white possessive property, power, and indigenous sovereignty*. University of Minnesota Press. http://www.jstor.org/stable/https://doi.org/10.5749/j.ctt155jmpf

Murray, S. A., Kendall, M., Carduff, E., Worth, A., Harris, F. M., Lloyd, A., Cavers, D., Grant, L., & Sheikh, A. (2009). Use of serial qualitative interviews to understand patients evolving experiences and needs. *British Medical Journal: BMJ, 339*(7727), 958–960. https://doi.org/10.1136/bmj.b3702

Nakata, M. (2007). *Disciplining the savages, savaging the disciplines*. Aboriginal Studies Press.

Povey, R., Trudgett, M., Page, S., & Locke, M. L. (2022a). Hidden in plain view: Indigenous early career researchers' experiences and perceptions of racism in Australian universities. *Critical Studies in Education, 64*(4), 355–373. https://doi.org/10.1080/17508487.2022.2159469

Povey, R., Trudgett, M., Page, S., Locke, M. L., & Harry, M. (2022b). Raising an Indigenous academic community: A strength-based approach to Indigenous early career mentoring in higher education. *The Australian Educational Researcher*. https://doi.org/10.1007/s13384-022-00542-3

Proud, A. D., & Morgan, A. (2021). Critical self-reflection. A foundational skill. In M. Shay & R. Oliver (Eds.), *Indigenous education in Australia. Learning and teaching for deadly futures* (pp. 39–50). Routledge.

Rigney, L.-I. (2001). A first perspective of indigenous Australian participation in science: Framing indigenous research towards indigenous Australian intellectual sovereignty. *Kaurna Higher Education Journal, 7*, 1–13.

Smith, A., Funaki, H., & MacDonald, L. (2021). Living, breathing settler-colonialism: The reification of settler norms in a common university space. *Higher Education Research and Development, 40*(1), 132–145. https://doi.org/10.1080/07294360.2020.1852190

Thunig, A., & Jones, T. (2020). 'Don't make me play house-n***er': Indigenous academic women treated as 'black performer' within higher education. *Australian Educational Researcher, 48*, 397–417. https://doi.org/10.1007/s13384-020-00405-9

Uink, B., Bennett, R., & van den Berg, C. (2021). Factors that enable Australian Aboriginal women's persistence at university: A strengths-based approach. *Higher Education Research and Development, 40*(1), 178–193. https://doi.org/10.1080/07294360.2020.1852185

Yunkaporta, T., & Shillingsworth, D. (2020) Relationally responsive standpoint. *Journal of Indigenous Research, 8*(4), https://doi.org/10.26077/ky71-qt27

Dr. Michelle Locke is a Boorooberongal woman of the Dharug Nation, a very proud Mum of two boys and Western Sydney University alumnus. From Jan 2020 to Dec 2022 Michelle was employed firstly as a Professional Researcher and following conferral of her Ph.D. in 2021 as a Postdoctoral Research Fellow with the Office of Deputy Vice-Chancellor Indigenous Leadership on the *Developing Indigenous Early Career Researchers* ARC project. In January 2023 Michelle commenced in the position of Senior Lecturer in the School of Education at Western Sydney University.

Open Access This chapter is licensed under the terms of the Creative Commons Attribution 4.0 International License (http://creativecommons.org/licenses/by/4.0/), which permits use, sharing, adaptation, distribution and reproduction in any medium or format, as long as you give appropriate credit to the original author(s) and the source, provide a link to the Creative Commons license and indicate if changes were made.

The images or other third party material in this chapter are included in the chapter's Creative Commons license, unless indicated otherwise in a credit line to the material. If material is not included in the chapter's Creative Commons license and your intended use is not permitted by statutory regulation or exceeds the permitted use, you will need to obtain permission directly from the copyright holder.

The manufacturer's authorised representative in the EU is Springer Nature Customer Service Centre GmbH, Europaplatz 3, 69115 Heidelberg, Germany. If you have any concerns regarding our products, please contact ProductSafety@springernature.com

Printed and bound by CPI Group (UK) Ltd, Croydon, CR0 4YY

25/03/2026

02078193-0018